The NEWFOUNDLAND and LABRADOR SEAFOOD COOKBOOK

JOAN ▪ OVER

The NEWFOUNDLAND and LABRADOR SEAFOOD COOKBOOK

BREAKWATER BOOKS

BREAKWATER
100 Water Street
P.O. Box 2188
St. John's, NL
A1C 6E6

National Library of Canada Cataloguing in Publication

Over, Joan
        The Newfoundland and Labrador seafood cookbook / Joan Over.

Includes index.

ISBN 1-55081-198-3

I. Cookery (Seafood) 2. Cookery--Newfoundland and Labrador.

TX747.O94 2003   641.6'9   C2003-903331-7

© 2003 Joan Over

Design & Layout: Rhonda Molloy, Carola Kern
Cover Design: Rhonda Molloy

The Canada Council | Le Conseil des Arts
for the Arts | du Canada

We acknowledge the financial support of The Canada Council for the Arts for our publishing activities.

We acknowledge the financial support of the Government of Canada
through the Book Publishing Industry Development Program (BPIDP) for
our publishing activities.

Printed in Canada.

TABLE OF CONTENTS

ACKNOWLEDGEMENTS

I owe a large debt of gratitude to my cousin, Dorothy Over-Keough, for her drawings. Dorothy grew up in a Newfoundland fishing community and is married to a commercial fisherman. Her knowledge of fish and shellfish anatomy and her talents as an artist have greatly enhanced my introductions to the various species.

I would also like to thank the many relatives and friends who contributed recipes, suggested recipes to be included in this book or offered their support in other ways.

Special thanks go to my mother and Nick Donovan for tips on freezing fish and to Nigel Allen of the Marine Institute of Memorial University of Newfoundland for information about sharks.

The largest portion of my gratitude is reserved for my husband, John King, who brought home his catch for the table, tasted and tested recipes, and enthusiastically provided support, advice and encouragement.

INTRODUCTION

More than anything else, the bounty of the sea has shaped the culture of Newfoundland and Labrador. For most of its history, this newest province of Canada was a colony of England and most of its people were engaged in the fishery. For almost five hundred years, northern Atlantic cod dominated that industry, but many other species—herring, capelin, turbot, lobster, just to name a few—have always been important both for commercial trade and personal consumption.

The drastic decline of the once-prolific cod, and the moratorium imposed on the cod fishery in 1992, had a profound impact on Newfoundland's economy and culture. For centuries, it was possible for hundreds of little communities to survive on inshore fishing from small boats. Many of these "outports" had no road connections to the rest of the province. On the Labrador coast, some small settlements were occupied only during the summer by fishermen who came from the island of Newfoundland every year to fish. Since the cod moratorium, many of the tiny isolated communities have disappeared. Much of the present-day fishery, such as the harvesting of scallops and shrimp, requires much bigger boats that go hundreds of miles offshore, and now the population tends to be concentrated in larger centres.

Still, when you travel around Newfoundland and Labrador, even today, you cannot help being struck by how the harvesting of seafood is an essential part of the province's way of life. In coastal communities, much of the talk is about fishing. Even a newcomer is quickly drawn into conversation about various kinds of fishing boats, which species are still being caught, what price they are fetching and who is buying them.

I grew up on conversations about fishing and meals that more often than not included some kind of seafood. Both my grandfathers were Newfoundland fishermen. One of them fished from a small dory in Bonavista Bay, where he dried and salted cod and processed lobster and squid for export. My other grandfather travelled with a crew during the summer to fish from his larger schooners off the coast of Labrador.

When I was growing up, I was aware only of the species of seafood caught by my relatives or available locally. Now, with the marvels of modern processing, refrigeration and transportation, I can go to the supermarket and make my choice from dozens of different varieties.

In this book, I've made no attempt to discuss every variety of seafood caught in Newfoundland waters. They are too numerous to all be included, and some of them are processed only for foreign markets. The species I've presented here are mainly those commonly accessible in fish markets and supermarkets across North America.

While there are many traditional Newfoundland and Labrador recipes in this book, I have not confined myself to those. Rather, I've tried to provide delicious ways to prepare certain species of seafood found around our coast with methods and ingredients that maximize their character and taste.

Some of these recipes are quite simple. Others are more complex. Some include ingredients that may not be readily available and sometimes I've made suggestions for substitutions.

I believe you should never feel bound to a recipe unless it involves a basic principle or technique. If your senses and imagination tell you that an ingredient or an amount would not be right for you, adjust it to suit your taste. Flexibility and learning to trust one's own instincts are essential to good cooking.

I cannot overstress the importance of the freshest ingredients possible, however. That goes not just for the seafood itself—it must always be very fresh or properly frozen—but also for all other components of the recipe. The ultimate quality of any dish is determined initially by the value of the ingredients and then by the time and effort the cook expends to handle and prepare them to bring out the best of their flavour.

It's also important not to overcook seafood. It is naturally tender and delicate and toughens easily. In most cases, it is done when it loses its translucent appearance or flakes easily.

Fish and shellfish are healthy food choices. They are generally low in fat and contain many essential vitamins and minerals. But my philosophy is that food should nourish life at more than just the maintenance level. It should look good, smell good and taste good. It should tempt your family and guests to truly take delight in the pleasures of the table.

With this book, my wish is to introduce some readers to the possibilities for cooking seafood, to renew the enthusiasm for seafood cookery for others, and to depict some of the wonders of the sea that surrounds Newfoundland and Labrador.

SEAFOOD STORAGE AND HANDLING

Fresh seafood should have a faint sea odour, but should not smell "fishy". Whole fish should have clear eyes, not filmed and dull. The gills should be red, not a faded greyish pink. The skin should glisten and the flesh should be firm and springy to the touch, not spongy. Cut fish, shelled crustacean meats and shucked mollusc meats should be moist, not slimy or dried around the edges.

Ideally, seafood should be purchased the day it is to be used because it is highly perishable. Of course, that's not always possible, so care must be taken to adequately and appropriately refrigerate or freeze it until it is prepared and cooked.

Store fresh seafood in the coldest part of your refrigerator (usually the lowest shelf at the back or in the meat keeper). Don't suffocate live lobsters, clams, mussels or oysters by sealing them in a plastic bag. They need to breathe. They're best kept in a bowl, covered with damp paper towels.

Before cooking, check that lobsters are still moving. Make sure clams and mussels are still alive by tapping any open shells. Discard those with shells that do not close.

Fish steaks or fillets, shrimp, scallop meat, crabmeat and lobster tails can be placed in sealed plastic storage bags or covered plastic containers and kept on ice in the refrigerator (32° to 34°F) for two or three days.

Whole fresh fish with skin and crustaceans in the shell, such as crab, lobster and shrimp, can be frozen in water and stored in the freezer at 0°F or lower for about three months. Do not freeze fish fillets or shelled seafood meat in water because juices will seep into the water during thawing and essential nutrients and flavour will be lost.

Never thaw seafood on the counter at room temperature. Allow one day to defrost frozen seafood in the refrigerator. If pressed for time, place the original package in a plastic bag, place it in a pan and run cold water on it in the sink until it is thawed. When thawing fish frozen in a solid block of water, put the block under cold running water until the ice melts. If defrosting in the microwave, follow the manufacturer's directions and use the seafood immediately. Never refreeze seafood once it has thawed.

Marinades add great flavour to seafood. Always marinate seafood under refrigeration. Discard the used marinade because it contains raw juices in which bacteria grow quickly.

Always keep raw and cooked seafood separate to prevent bacterial contamination. After handling raw seafood, wash all utensils, cutting surfaces and your hands with hot soapy water.

Note on Measurement

The metric system has been used in Canada for many years, but because many people have retained older recipes and many cookbooks are imported from the United States (which does not use the metric system), most cooks are more familiar with teaspoons and pounds than with millilitres and grams. Therefore this book is in imperial measurement. For those who wish to use metric measurement, however, a conversion table is given here. These are approximate equivalents that should give the same results in cooking.

Imperial measures	Metric measures
1 teaspoon	5 millilitres
1 tablespoon	15 millilitres
¼ cup	50 millilitres
⅓ cup	75 millilitres
½ cup	100 millilitres
⅔ cup	150 millilitres
¾ cup	175 millilitres
1 cup	200 millilitres
1 ounce	30 grams
¼ pound	125 grams
½ pound	250 grams
1 pound	500 grams

ATLANTIC COD

Cod is, hands down, my favourite fish. Perhaps that's mainly because I'm a Newfoundlander, but there are other reasons. When cod is very fresh, the meat is delicate and sweet like no other. And cod is versatile. It's excellent baked, broiled, pan-fried or poached and is wonderful in stews and chowders.

Historically, cod has been Newfoundland's most important fish, both as food and as a major resource in world trade. It was the bountiful North Atlantic cod supply that led to Newfoundland's discovery and settlement. For centuries, almost the entire population of Newfoundland was at the mercy of cod fishery, how many could be caught and what price they would fetch. Whole families lived by fishing, splitting, salting and drying cod for distant markets and their own most staple sustenance.

After the abrupt collapse of stocks early in the 1990s, a moratorium was placed on the Newfoundland cod fishery and now catches are substantially reduced in an effort to protect the species.

Atlantic cod, *gadus morhua*, are found in both inshore and offshore waters all around Newfoundland and Labrador. They are bottom feeders, inhabiting marine shelves where the water is cold. They have a "sound", or swim bladder, an organ that adjusts to give them the same weight as the surrounding water, allowing them buoyancy without having to use their fins. The sound itself is edible. It has a texture similar to beef tripe and is prized by many Newfoundlanders as a tasty morsel.

Commercially caught cod are from about two to five pounds in weight, although they have been known to grow up to more than 200 pounds.

Cod meat is snowy white, very lean and firm, but with a tender texture. When cooked, it falls apart into large flakes.

Cod cheeks and tongues are both considered delicacies in Newfoundland. The texture of the tongue is soft, something like that of a scallop, but the cheeks have quite firm meat, even after cooking.

Dried salt cod has been heavily salted to extract the moisture and help to preserve the fish. Before cooking, it must be soaked well to remove most of the salt.

COD CHOWDER

6 SERVINGS

- ¼ pound salt fat pork, cut into ¼-inch dice
- 2 medium-sized onions, thinly sliced
- A 2½- to 3-pound cleaned fresh cod, with head removed and reserved and the body cut into thick slices
- 3 cups cold water
- 3 medium-sized boiling potatoes, cut into ½-inch dice
- 2 teaspoons salt
- Freshly ground black pepper
- 3 cups milk
- 2 tablespoons butter

Newfoundlanders prize the cod's head for chowder. If you don't have the head, you should add some fish bones to give the chowder its traditional gelatinous consistency. Soda crackers, crushed and sprinkled on top, are the usual accompaniment.

In a heavy 4- to 5- quart pot, fry the salt pork dice over moderate heat, turning them frequently until they are crisp and have rendered all their fat. Add the onions and cook, stirring occasionally, for about 5 minutes or until they are soft but not brown.

Add the cod's head to the pot. Pour in the water and bring the mixture to a boil over high heat, skimming off the foam. Add the potatoes, the salt and a generous grinding of black pepper. Reduce the heat to low, partially cover the pot and simmer for 20 minutes. Add the slices of fish and continue to simmer, partially covered, for about 15 minutes longer or until the potatoes are tender and the fish flakes easily.

Remove the cod's head from the pot and discard it. With tongs or a slotted spoon, remove the slices of fish and transfer them to a large plate or platter. Remove the skin and bones from the fish and discard them. Cut the fish into bite-sized pieces and return it to the pot.

Add the milk and butter and, stirring gently, bring the mixture to a simmer over moderately low heat. Do not let it boil.

Taste and adjust the seasonings and add a little more water or milk if the chowder seems too thick.

To serve, ladle the chowder into a heated soup tureen or individual soup plates.

Pan-Fried Cod Fillets

4 to 6 Servings

- 2 pounds fresh boneless cod fillets
- ¾ cup all-purpose flour
- ¾ teaspoon salt
- ¼ teaspoon freshly ground black pepper
- 3 tablespoons butter
- 3 tablespoons vegetable oil

Other fish are called by their names, "salmon" or "herring", for example, but if a Newfoundlander just says "fish", it means cod.

The fish for this traditional Newfoundland recipe should be very fresh. The fillets may be served with tartar sauce or simply garnished with lemon wedges. Boiled potatoes are the usual accompaniment.

Pat the cod fillets completely dry with paper towels. In a large shallow dish or deep platter, mix together the flour, salt and pepper. Roll the fillets around in the flour mixture to coat them evenly and shake off any excess.

In a large heavy frying pan, heat the butter and oil together over moderate heat. When the foam subsides, add the cod fillets, a few at a time. Do not crowd the pan. Regulating the heat so the fillets do not scorch, fry them for 4 to 6 minutes on each side (depending on their thickness), turning them carefully with a wide spatula.

The fillets are done when they flake easily when prodded gently with a fork. When the fillets are cooked, remove them to a heated platter and keep them warm in a low oven while you fry the remaining fillets in the same manner. Serve as soon as all the fillets are cooked.

WHOLE BAKED STUFFED COD
6 TO 8 SERVINGS

- ¼ pound salt pork fat, cut into ¼-inch dice
- 3 cups soft bread crumbs, made from homemade-type white bread
- 1 medium-sized onion, finely chopped
- 1 tablespoon dried summer savory
- ½ teaspoon salt
- Freshly ground black pepper
- 4 tablespoons butter, melted
- A 4- to 5- pound whole fresh cod, cleaned and with the backbone removed, but with the head and tail left on
- 1 medium-sized onion, thickly sliced
- Lemon wedges and sprigs of parsley for garnish

I've heard a whole stuffed cod referred to as "Newfoundland turkey". My grandmother certainly considered it grand enough for a special occasion. This is her recipe, passed on to me by my aunt.

In an enamelled or stainless steel roasting or baking pan, large enough to hold the fish comfortably, fry the salt pork dice on the top of the stove over moderate heat, turning them about frequently with a slotted spoon until they are crisp and brown and have rendered all their fat. Scoop out the pork dice with the slotted spoon and discard them. Set the pan aside, with the fat remaining in it.

Preheat the oven to 400°F. In a large mixing bowl, combine the bread crumbs, chopped onion, savory, salt and a generous grinding of black pepper. Stir in the melted butter and toss together well.

Wash the fish and dry it well, inside and out. Fill the fish cavity loosely with the bread stuff-ing. Close the opening with small skewers and crisscross with kitchen string as you would to lace a turkey.

Place the fish in the roasting pan and baste it all over with some of the fat. Bake the fish for 30 minutes, uncovered, basting every 10 minutes or so with the fat accumulated in the pan.

Scatter the slices of onion over and around the fish and continue to bake, basting occasionally, for 30 minutes longer. The fish should be firm when lightly pressed.

Remove the pan from the oven. Using two wide spatulas, carefully transfer the fish to a heated serving platter and remove the skewers and string. Serve the fish garnished with lemon wedges and sprigs of parsley.

COD AU GRATIN
4 SERVINGS

There are numerous recipes for this very popular dish that you will find on the menus of most Newfoundland and Labrador restaurants. This is my own rich version.

- 4 tablespoons butter
- ½ cup finely chopped onions
- 2 tablespoons flour
- 1 cup light cream or half and half
- 1 teaspoon salt
- ¼ teaspoon pepper
- 1½ cups grated sharp cheddar cheese
- 1 teaspoon lemon juice
- 1½ pounds fresh cod fillets, or frozen fillets thoroughly defrosted

Preheat the oven to 350°F. Use 1 tablespoon of the butter to evenly grease the bottom and sides of a shallow 2-quart baking dish.

In a large heavy saucepan, melt the remaining 3 tablespoons of butter over moderate heat. Add the onions and, stirring frequently, cook them for about 5 minutes, or until they are soft but not brown. Stir in the flour and blend well. Then, whisking the mixture constantly, pour in the cream in a thin stream and continue to cook and stir over moderate heat until the sauce comes to a boil and is thick and smooth. Stir in the salt, pepper and 1 cup of the grated cheese. When the cheese has completely melted, stir in the lemon juice.

Pat the cod fillets completely dry with paper towels and cut each of them into 2 or 3 pieces.

Pour a thin layer of the sauce evenly over the bottom of the prepared baking dish. Cover the sauce with half the fish fillets. Cover the fillets with another thin layer of sauce. Lay the remaining fillets on top and pour the rest of the sauce evenly over all. Sprinkle the remaining ½ cup of grated cheese over the top. Bake the fish for about 25 minutes or until the sauce is hot and bubbling. If you wish, you may slide the dish under the broiler for a minute or so to brown the top lightly. Serve directly from the baking dish.

COD AND RICE CASSEROLE
4 SERVINGS

- ¾ cup raw long-grain rice
- 1 teaspoon salt
- 3 tablespoons unsalted butter
- 2 medium-sized onions, very thinly sliced
- 2 large cloves garlic, minced
- 1 teaspoon dried summer savory
- 1 pound cod fillets, only partially defrosted if frozen
- Freshly ground black pepper
- 1 tablespoon freshly squeezed lemon juice
- 1 7½-ounce can of tomato sauce
- 1 cup grated mozzarella cheese
- 2 tablespoons freshly grated parmesan cheese

This is one of my most requested recipes and a dish that houseguests have come to expect for a luncheon during their visit. It's my favourite recipe for frozen cod fillets because, if they are only partially defrosted, enough so that you can pull them apart easily, the cod doesn't overcook in the oven.

In a small saucepan, combine the rice with 1½ cups of water and ¾ teaspoon salt. Bring the mixture to a boil over high heat, reduce the heat to low, cover the saucepan and cook for 12 minutes. The rice will finish cooking in the oven.

Meanwhile, in a 10-inch heavy frying pan, melt the butter over moderately low heat. Add the onions and garlic and, stirring frequently, cook them for 7-8 minutes or until they are soft but not brown.

Preheat the oven to 375°F. Scrape the onions, along with any butter remaining in the frying pan, into a shallow 1½-quart casserole dish and spread them evenly over the bottom.

Cover the onions with the rice-and-water mixture and sprinkle with the savory. Cut the cod fillets into manageable-sized pieces that will fit to the edges of the dish. Lay them as evenly as possible over the rice. Sprinkle the fish with the remaining ¼ teaspoon salt, a generous grinding of pepper and the lemon juice. Pour the tomato sauce over the fish and, using the back of a spoon, spread it to the edges of the dish. Cover the top evenly with the grated mozzarella cheese and sprinkle on the parmesan cheese.

Bake the casserole for 30 minutes, uncovered, or until the cheese bubbles and begins to brown. Serve directly from the baking dish.

COD PROVENÇALE
4 SERVINGS

- ½ cup all-purpose flour
- ½ teaspoon salt
- Freshly ground black pepper
- 1½ pounds thick cod fillets, cut into 2½-inch pieces
- 2 tablespoons unsalted butter
- 2 tablespoons olive oil
- 1½ cups finely chopped onions
- 2 cloves garlic, minced
- 4 medium-sized firm vine-ripened tomatoes, quartered and seeded
- 12 large ripe black olives, preferably packed in brine, pitted
- 1 lemon, cut into 8 wedges
- 2 tablespoons finely chopped fresh parsley leaves

The first time I made this dish for my husband, he was so impressed with its colourful appearance that he took a picture of the platter. But there's more to this than a pretty presentation; the combination of flavours is superb. I like to serve the fish with thick rounds of potatoes sautéed in olive oil.

Preheat the oven to a low temperature and place a large oven-proof platter in it.

Put the flour, salt and a few grindings of black pepper in a large paper or plastic bag. Shake the cod in the bag, a few pieces at a time, until the pieces are well coated. Shake off the excess flour.

In a large heavy frying pan over moderate heat, melt the butter together with the olive oil. When the foam subsides, add the onions and garlic and cook, stirring occasionally, until they are golden brown, about 7 or 8 minutes. With a slotted spoon, remove the onions and garlic from the pan and spread them evenly over the heated platter. Return the platter to the oven.

Add the pieces of cod, a few at a time, to the fat remaining in the pan and fry them over moderate heat, turning them frequently, until they are golden brown on all sides, about 4 or 5 minutes. As each batch of fish is cooked, remove the pieces from the pan and place them over the onions and garlic, returning the platter to the oven.

When all the fish is cooked, add the tomatoes and olives to the frying pan and cook them over low heat, stirring occasionally and gently, for 3 or 4 minutes, or until they are heated through. Arrange the tomatoes and olives attractively over the pieces of fish. Surround the edge of the platter with the lemon wedges and sprinkle with the parsley.

Cod with Tomatoes and Prunes
4 Servings

- 3 tablespoons olive oil
- 2 large cloves garlic, peeled
- ¾ cup dry sherry
- 1½ cups canned plum tomatoes with juice, coarsely chopped
- ¾ teaspoon salt
- Freshly ground black pepper
- 4 thick cod fillets or cod loins, thoroughly defrosted if frozen (about 2 pounds total)
- ¼ cup diced pitted prunes
- 2 tablespoons finely chopped parsley

One of the first meals my husband cooked for me was cod with a rice dish that included marinated dried apricots. That's when I discovered that dried fruit and cod make great companions.

In a large frying pan, heat the oil over moderate heat. Add the garlic and cook, stirring, until it is golden brown on all sides. Using a slotted spoon, remove and discard the garlic. (It is used only to flavour the oil.)

Add the sherry to the pan and boil it for 3 or 4 minutes, or until it is reduced by half. Add the tomatoes with their juice, the salt and a generous grinding of pepper. Bring the mixture to a boil. Add the cod, reduce the heat to low, partially cover the frying pan and cook for 10 to 12 minutes, or until the cod flakes easily with a fork. Gently remove the cod and place the pieces on a platter or 4 individual plates. Keep the fish warm in a low oven while you finish the sauce.

Add the prunes and parsley to the mixture remaining in the frying pan and simmer slowly for about 3 minutes. Taste for seasoning and add more salt if necessary. Spoon the sauce over the fish and serve immediately.

DEEP-FRIED COD CHEEKS
6 SERVINGS

Cod cheeks, sometimes called "fish faces" or "sculps", are a special Newfoundland delicacy.

- 2 eggs
- ¾ cup milk
- 1 teaspoon salt
- Freshly ground black pepper
- 2 pounds very fresh cod cheeks, rinsed and patted dry
- Vegetable oil for deep frying
- 1 cup all-purpose flour
- Lemon wedges

In a deep bowl, beat the eggs until they are frothy. Add the milk, the salt and a generous grinding of black pepper and mix well. Drop the cod cheeks into the mixture and turn them with a spoon to coat them evenly.

Pour the vegetable oil into a heavy pot or deep fryer to a depth of about 3 inches. Heat the oil until it is very hot, but not smoking (about 375°F on a deep-frying thermometer).

Meanwhile, preheat the oven to its lowest setting. Line a large baking sheet with paper towels and place it in the middle of the oven.

Spread the flour out on a large piece of waxed paper. When the oil is hot, pick up the soaked cod cheeks, a few at a time, shake off the excess liquid and roll them in the flour until they are evenly coated on all sides. Drop the floured cheeks, a few at a time, into the hot oil. Do not crowd them. Fry the cheeks for about 5 minutes, or until they are golden brown, turning them frequently. As each batch is fried, transfer it with a skimmer or slotted spoon to the paper-lined baking sheet to keep warm while you fry the rest. Make sure the oil returns to 375°F between each batch.

When all the cod cheeks are fried, serve them hot, garnished with the lemon wedges.

FRIED COD TONGUES
4 SERVINGS

Yes, cod do have tongues and they're delicious. They are usually served with mashed potatoes or French fries.

- 1 pound fresh cod tongues
- 1 tablespoon freshly squeezed lemon juice
- ¾ cup all-purpose flour
- ½ teaspoon salt
- Freshly ground black pepper
- ¼ pound salt fat pork, cut into ¼-inch dice
- Tartar sauce (see recipe index)

Wash the tongues under cold water and pat them dry. Lay the tongues side by side on a piece of waxed paper and sprinkle them as evenly as possible with the lemon juice.

In a large paper or plastic bag, combine the flour, salt and a few grindings of black pepper.

In a large heavy frying pan, fry the salt pork dice over moderate heat, turning them frequently, until they are crisp and have rendered all their fat. Scoop them out of the pan with a slotted spoon and reserve them on a dish lined with paper towel. Leave the fat in the pan.

Reheat the pork fat until it is very hot but not smoking. Drop the cod tongues into the flour mixture in the bag. Shake the bag to coat the tongues evenly on all sides. Shake any excess flour from the tongues and arrange them in one layer in the hot fat. Fry the tongues, uncovered, over moderately low heat for about 10 minutes on each side, or until they are golden brown.

Drain the cod tongues quickly on paper towels and arrange them on a heated platter or individual plates, garnished, if you wish, with the reserved salt pork dice. Serve tartar sauce in a small bowl to be passed separately.

Salt Cod Brandade
About 8 Appetizer Servings

- 1 pound salt cod, skinned and boned
- 3 cups water
- ½ teaspoon fennel seeds
- 6 cloves garlic, unpeeled but crushed
- 1 large bay leaf
- ¼ cup extra-virgin olive oil
- 3 tablespoons heavy cream

Brandade is a specialty from the south of France that has gained popularity almost anywhere salt cod is available. It is usually spread on toasted slices of baguette as a first course or to accompany drinks before dinner. It may be made a day ahead of time, covered and refrigerated, but let it come to room temperature before serving.

The best salt cod for this recipe is taken from just behind the abdomen, where it is thickest.

Beginning the night before you wish to serve the brandade, place the salt cod in a deep bowl and cover it with cold water. Soak the cod for at least 18 hours, changing the water once or twice.

In a medium-sized heavy saucepan, combine the water, fennel seeds, garlic and bay leaf. Bring the mixture to a boil, reduce the heat to low and simmer, covered, for 30 minutes. Add the salt cod to the saucepan and bring it to a boil. Turn off the heat, but leave the salt cod on the stove to poach in the cooling liquid for about 30 minutes. Drain the fish, discarding the poaching liquid, and cut it into small pieces.

In two small saucepans, heat the olive oil and the cream separately until they reach a simmer. Do not let them boil. Keep the oil and cream hot.

In a food processor, process the pieces of salt cod for a few seconds. Pour in about 1 tablespoon of the hot olive oil and process again. Repeat the process with 2 more tablespoons of the oil. Then, in the same manner, pulse in 2 tablespoons of the cream. At this point, the brandade should be creamy and have just the right consistency for spreading. If it appears too thick, pulse in a little more olive oil and cream.

Taste the brandade for seasoning and transfer it to a serving bowl. If storing it in the refrigerator, cover tightly.

SALT COD RAVIOLI IN BISQUE
6 FIRST-COURSE SERVINGS

This takes a little work, but the effort is certainly worth it.

- 18 wonton wrappers, thawed if frozen
- 1 cup salt cod brandade (see recipe index)
- ¼ cup olive oil
- 2 large vine-ripened tomatoes
- 1 large onion, chopped
- 2 large cloves garlic, minced
- 2 medium-sized carrots chopped
- 1 large celery stalk, chopped
- 4 cups basic fish stock (see recipe index)

- 4 cups cold water
- 1½ cups dry white wine
- 2 tablespoons cognac, or other good French brandy
- 1 teaspoon fennel seeds, crushed
- ½ teaspoon ground coriander or ground coriander seeds
- 1 bay leaf
- 10 whole black peppercorns
- 2 teaspoons salt

Put 1 wonton wrapper on a lightly floured surface and mound 1 level tablespoon of brandade in the centre. Brush the edges of the wrapper with water and fold it in half to form a triangle, pressing around the filling to force out air. Transfer the ravioli to a baking sheet lined with waxed paper. Make more ravioli with the remaining wrappers and brandade in the same manner. When all the ravioli are made, cover them with plastic wrap and refrigerate until ready to cook. They may be made up to 2 hours ahead of time.

In a large heavy saucepan, heat the olive oil over moderate heat. Add the tomatoes, onion, garlic, carrots and celery, and cook, stirring frequently, until they are soft but not brown. Stir in the stock, water, wine, cognac, spices and salt. Bring the mixture to a simmer, and simmer, uncovered, for 25 minutes.

Pour the bisque through a fine sieve set over a large bowl, pressing down hard on the solids to extract all their juices. Discard the solids. Return the bisque to the saucepan.

Bring it to a boil and boil until it is reduced to 4 cups. Taste and adjust the seasonings. Keep the bisque hot over low heat.

In a large pot of boiling water, cook the ravioli gently in 2 batches for 6 to 8 minutes or until they rise to surface and are tender. As the ravioli are cooked, use a slotted spoon to transfer 3 of them to each of 6 heated soup plates. Pour the hot bisque over the ravioli and serve immediately.

FISH CAKES
ABOUT 6 SERVINGS

- 2 pounds salt cod, skinned and boned
- 8 medium-sized boiling potatoes, peeled and cut into quarters
- 1 tablespoon butter
- ¾ cup finely chopped onions
- ¼ teaspoon freshly ground black pepper
- 1 teaspoon dried summer savory (optional)
- ½ cup all-purpose flour
- ¼ pound salt pork fat, rind removed, cut into ¼-inch dice

I've often watched my mother make fish cakes, forming them all into patties of the same size and frying them to crusty goldenness in pork fat. Like most Newfoundlanders, I now make these almost weekly.

Beginning the night before you wish to serve the fish cakes, place the salt cod in a deep bowl and cover it with cold water. Soak the cod for at least 18 hours, changing the water once or twice.

Drain the fish and cut it into pieces. Place the fish in a large non-reactive saucepan. Cover it with cold water and bring it to a boil over high heat. Reduce the heat to low, cover and simmer for about 20 minutes or until the fish flakes easily. At the same time, in a separate saucepan, boil the potatoes in lightly salted water until they are quite tender. Drain the fish and the potatoes thoroughly and separate the fish into flakes.

In a large bowl, mash the hot potatoes with the butter. Stir in the onions, pepper and savory (if you wish). Add the fish and combine well.

Line a large baking sheet with waxed paper. Put the flour on another large piece of waxed paper. Scoop up a handful of the fish and potato mixture and, using your fingers, pat and shape it into a flat cake, about 3 inches in diameter and ¾ inch thick. Dip each cake in the flour to coat it evenly on all sides, shaking off any excess. Place each flour-coated cake on the paper-lined baking sheet and continue to shape and coat the cakes until all the fish-and-potato mixture has been used. Refrigerate the fish cakes for at least 1 hour.

In a large heavy frying pan, fry the salt pork dice over moderate heat, turning them frequently, until they are crisp and have rendered all their fat. Scoop the pork dice out of the pan with a slotted spoon and discard them.

In the fat remaining in the pan, fry 3 or 4 cakes at a time, over moderate heat for about 5 minutes per side, turning only once, until they are crusty and well-browned. As they are done transfer them to a platter and keep them warm in a low oven until all the remaining cakes are fried.

FISH AND BREWIS
4 TO 6 SERVINGS

- 1½ pounds salt cod, skinned and boned
- 4 cakes hard bread (also called hard tack)
- ¼ pound salt pork fat, rind removed, cut into ¼-inch dice
- 1 small onion, finely chopped

Fish and brewis (pronounced "brews") is Newfoundland's most distinctive dish. There are numerous regional recipes for it and arguments abound about whether it is best made with fresh or salt cod. Made with salt fish, this is my family's traditional recipe. We serve it with boiled potatoes.

Beginning the night before you wish to serve the fish and brewis, place the salt cod in a deep bowl and cover it with cold water. Soak the cod for at least 18 hours, changing the water once or twice.

Split the cakes of hard bread in half and place them in a large bowl. Fill the bowl with cold water to within ½ inch of its brim and place a large heavy plate over it. Soak the bread for the same length of time as the fish, but do not change the water. (The plate will ensure that the bread is submerged in the water to soften completely. It will swell to almost twice its original size.)

About 45 minutes before you wish to serve the meal, drain the fish and rinse it under cold running water. Place it in a large non-reactive saucepan, cover it with cold water and bring it to a boil over high heat. Reduce the heat to low, cover and simmer for about 20 minutes or until the fish flakes easily. Drain the fish and return it to the pot to keep it warm.

Meanwhile, in a heavy frying pan, fry the salt pork dice over moderate heat, turning them about frequently until they begin to brown. Add the onion and continue to fry, stirring occasionally, until the onion is brown and the pork dice are crisp and have rendered all their fat. (The fried pork dice are called "scrunchions".) Set the contents of the frying pan aside.

Transfer the hard bread and its soaking water to a large heavy pot. Bring the bread and water to a boil over high heat. Immediately remove the pot from the heat and drain the bread thoroughly in a large colander. Return the bread to the pot and chop it into small pieces with the edge of a large spoon. Cut the fish into small pieces (or coarsely flake it with a fork) and add it to the bread, mixing them together thoroughly.

Transfer the fish and brewis to a large heated serving platter. Reheat the contents of the scrunchion pan briefly and spoon it into a small heated sauceboat. Serve at once. Each diner ladles some of the scrunchions, onion and melted pork fat over a serving of fish and brewis.

ATLANTIC SALMON

There are many places in Newfoundland and Labrador where you can watch a salmon leap on its homeward-bound journey and observe its incredible strength, grace and beauty. Atlantic salmon, *salmo salar*, are anadromous, which means they are born in fresh water and migrate to the sea to grow and mature. Then they return to the same river where they were born, propelling themselves against the current and up waterfalls, to spawn.

An angler's paradise, Newfoundland and Labrador boasts 177 scheduled salmon rivers, almost all of them uncrowded and with pristine waters in peaceful surroundings. Anyone with a licence is free to fish any stretch of river, although the number of salmon that may be retained is restricted and non-residents must be accompanied by a guide.

For centuries Atlantic salmon were considered little more than a nuisance, becoming entangled in nets and traps designed for other species. In the early 1900s, their economic value was recognized and a commercial salmon fishery existed in Newfoundland until the 1980s. Now, due to environmental problems and overfishing, wild salmon stocks are greatly reduced and all commercially sold Atlantic salmon are farmed or pen-raised.

Atlantic salmon have a dark back with silvery sides, more silvery if they're fresh from the sea. They have a smallish head and their upper body, head and fins are marked with small spots.

Salmon range in size from three to sixty pounds or more, and the range in quality and texture is almost as great, depending on how long they have been from the sea, their age, their diet and if they are wild or farmed. All salmon, however, have delicious pink firm flesh.

Salmon is always popular, whether simply prepared or served with a rich sauce. Barbecued salmon is a wonderful summer treat and nothing is quite so impressive on a buffet table as a whole glazed salmon. Just remember that careful cooking is important. Overcooked salmon is dry and loses flavour.

The quality and taste of smoked salmon varies from region to region, and even from smokehouse to smokehouse, depending on the smoking method. Generally, though, the salmon is first placed in brine to draw out the moisture and then smoked for several days over a hardwood fire. Properly processed, smoked salmon will keep, refrigerated, for several months.

SALMON MOUSSE
10 TO 16 SERVINGS

- Vegetable oil for greasing the mould
- 1 envelope (1 tablespoon) gelatin
- ¼ cup cold water
- ½ cup tomato juice, heated to a simmer
- 1 tablespoon finely chopped green onion
- 1½ cups cooked flaked salmon or canned salmon, well-drained
- 2 hard-cooked eggs, chopped
- 2 tablespoons sweet green pickle relish
- 1½ cups mayonnaise, preferably homemade (see recipe index)

I've been making this delicious mousse for more than thirty years. The recipe came from a friend named Elspeth and I sampled it for the first time when she included it as part of a buffet. The mousse may also be cut into slices and served on lettuce leaves as an appetizer or, because it's quite easy to spread, it may be served with crackers or thin slices of rye bread.

If I have a little smoked salmon left over from another preparation, I chop it finely and fold it into the mousse mixture for added flavour.

Lightly oil a 1-quart mould, terrine or loaf pan.

Sprinkle the gelatin on top of the cold water and let it stand for 5 minutes to soften. Add the gelatin to the heated tomato juice and stir until it is completely dissolved.

In a food processor or blender, combine the green onion, salmon, hard-cooked eggs and relish. Pulse the mixture until it is smooth. Scrape the mixture into a large bowl and, using a spatula, fold in the gelatin mixture and mayonnaise until no trace of white from the mayonnaise remains.

Spoon the mixture into the prepared mould, smoothing the top with a spoon. Cover and chill the mousse for at least 4 hours or until it is very firm.

Just before serving, run a thin knife around the edge of the mould. Dip the bottom of the mould in hot water for 5 to 10 seconds. Invert the mousse onto a platter or plate and garnish as desired.

WHOLE POACHED SALMON
8 SERVINGS

Whole poached salmon makes a very elegant main course.

- 1 5- to 6-pound whole salmon, cleaned, with backbone removed but skin, head and tail left intact
- 1 teaspoon salt
- ½ cup freshly squeezed lemon juice
- 1 large onion, coarsely chopped
- 2 carrots, coarsely chopped
- 2 celery stalks with leaves, coarsely chopped
- 1 large bay leaf
- 2 fresh thyme sprigs or ¼ teaspoon dried thyme
- 10 whole black peppercorns
- 1 pimiento-stuffed olive
- Lemon wedges
- Parsley sprigs

Wash the salmon inside and out and sprinkle the inside with the salt. Wrap the fish snugly in a double layer of cheesecloth and tie the ends securely with kitchen string, leaving the string long enough to serve as handles.

Place a fish poacher with a rack (or a roasting pan equipped with a rack and a lid) across 2 burners on the stovetop. Add the lemon juice, vegetables, herbs, peppercorns and 6 quarts of water. Bring the mixture to a boil. Using the string as handles, lower the salmon into the boiling liquid. Tie the string to the handles to facilitate lifting the salmon out of the poacher. The liquid should cover the salmon by 1 inch. If it does not, add boiling water.

Place the lid on the poacher or roasting pan. Bring the liquid to a simmer over moderate heat. Immediately reduce the heat to low. Simmer gently for 25 to 35 minutes or until the salmon feels firm when gently prodded with your finger. (Do not overcook.)

Untie the kitchen string from the poacher handles and use the string to lift the salmon onto a large cutting board or towel-covered work surface. Let the salmon rest for 10 minutes to firm up.

Have ready a large heated platter. Cut the string and open the cheesecloth. With a small sharp knife, peel the skin from the exposed surface of the body of the fish and scrape off and discard any grey fat. Holding both ends of the cheesecloth, carefully lift the salmon and turn it over onto the platter. Peel the skin and remove the fat from the second side.

To serve, place the olive in the eye cavity of the fish and garnish the salmon attractively with lemon slices and parsley sprigs.

GLAZED WHOLE SALMON
ABOUT 12 BUFFET SERVINGS

Glazed whole salmon is a bit of work, but it's always a buffet hit.

- 1 5- to 6-pound whole poached salmon (see recipe index)
- 1 cup dry white wine
- ¼ cup dry sherry
- 2 sprigs fresh thyme or ¼ teaspoon dried thyme
- 1 teaspoon salt
- 3 large eggs whites lightly beaten, egg shells reserved
- 1 tablespoon unflavored gelatin
- ¼ cup cold water
- Garnishes of choice (olive slices, lemon slices, parsley, etc.)

Follow the recipe for whole poached salmon just up to the point where it is cooked. Remove it from the heat and, still wrapped and in the poacher, let it cool, uncovered for 30 minutes. Refrigerate it in the poacher (do not unwrap the cheesecloth or pour off broth), uncovered, for at least 8 hours. Then, lift the salmon out of the broth and drain it. Transfer it, still wrapped in cheesecloth, to a large baking sheet and place it back in the refrigerator.

Pour the cooking broth through a sieve into a large bowl. Transfer 8 cups of the broth to a 4-quart heavy pot. (Reserve the remainder for another use.) Add the white wine, sherry, thyme and salt and boil until the liquid is reduced to 5 cups, about 30 to 40 minutes. Cool the broth for 30 minutes.

Remove the strings and open the cheesecloth. Following the directions in the whole poached salmon recipe, remove the skin and transfer the salmon to a cold, rather than heated, platter.

In a large heavy saucepan, combine the reduced broth, egg whites and egg shells.

Bring the mixture to a boil, whisking constantly. Reduce the heat and cook at a bare simmer, undisturbed, for 30 minutes. Carefully ladle the broth through a sieve lined with a double thickness of dampened cheesecloth set over a bowl. Discard the solids. Reserve the broth.

Soften the gelatin in cold water in a 1-quart saucepan for 1 minute. Add 3 cups of the broth and simmer, stirring, until the gelatin is dissolved.

Ladle this aspic into a metal bowl set in a larger bowl of ice water. Let it stand, stirring occasionally, until it is the consistency of raw egg white. Spoon a thin layer of aspic all over the salmon and chill it until the aspic is set, about 10 minutes. Arrange the chosen garnishes on the salmon and glaze it with more aspic. Chill the salmon for 10 more minutes. Repeat with another coating of aspic and keep the salmon chilled, uncovered, until ready to serve.

To serve, cut away and discard excess aspic and decorate as desired.

BARBECUED SALMON
ABOUT 6 SERVINGS

This recipe comes from my father-in-law, Chuck King. He's not only a great outdoor cook, but also an expert at filleting fish.

- 1 cup mesquite or hickory wood chips, soaked in hot water for 20 minutes
- Heavy-duty aluminum foil
- 1 salmon, about 5 pounds, filleted, with skin left on
- Cooking oil spray, or cooking oil
- ½ teaspoon garlic salt
- 1 lemon, cut into very thin slices
- 1 medium-sized onion, cut into very thin slices
- ¼ cup pimiento-stuffed olives, cut in half
- 2 tablespoons cold unsalted butter, cut into small bits
- ½ cup dry white wine
- ½ teaspoon paprika
- Sprigs of parsley for garnish

Preheat the barbecue to very hot. Loosely wrap the water-soaked hickory or mesquite chips in a double layer of the heavy foil and place them directly on the barbecue coals. (The top of the package should be open.)

Rinse the salmon fillets under cold running water and pat them dry with paper towels. Use a double layer of the heavy foil to form a 1½-inch deep pan large enough to hold the fillets. Fold and pinch to secure the corners and sides of the pan well. Spray the bottom of the pan with the cooking spray or brush it liberally with cooking oil. Place the pan on a large rimless tray or cutting board for support. Place the salmon fillets in the pan, skin side down.

Sprinkle the fillets evenly with the garlic salt. Arrange the slices of lemon and onion alternately over the fillets, decorating each fillet with olive halves, pimiento side up. Place the bits of butter between and around the lemon, onion and olives. Pour the wine into the bottom of the pan. Sprinkle the fillets evenly with the paprika.

Using a board for support, slide the foil pan onto the barbecue grill and reduce the heat to moderate. After 15 minutes, begin checking the salmon with a fork to see if it is beginning to flake. Once the salmon begins to flake, raise the heat to high. Using the tip of a very sharp knife, or a skewer, punch a few holes in the bottom of the pan. (This will enhance the smoke flavour.) Close the barbecue lid and allow the salmon to cook for 5 minutes longer.

To serve, lift the salmon fillets onto a heated platter or individual heated plates. Garnish the salmon with sprigs of parsley.

SEARED SALMON WITH BABY SPINACH
4 SERVINGS

I like to complete this delicious entrée with tiny boiled new potatoes and a cucumber salad.

- 4 6-ounce skinless salmon fillets
- Salt
- Freshly ground black pepper
- 3 tablespoons unsalted butter
- ½ cup thinly sliced shallots
- 2 tablespoons chopped fresh tarragon leaves
- 1 pound baby spinach leaves
- ¾ cup dry white wine
- ½ cup heavy cream

Sprinkle the salmon fillets with salt and pepper. In a large heavy frying pan over moderately high heat, melt 2 tablespoons of the butter. Add the salmon fillets and sauté them, turning once, until they are just opaque in the centre, about 4 minutes per side. Transfer the fillets to a platter and keep them warm in a low oven.

Add half of the shallots and half of the tarragon to the frying pan and sauté them, stirring, for about 1 minute. Increase the heat to high and add half of the spinach, tossing until wilted. Add the remaining spinach and toss until wilted. Divide the spinach mixture among 4 heated plates, spreading it out to form a bed for the fish.

Quickly melt the remaining tablespoon of butter in the same frying pan over moderately high heat. Add the remaining shallots and tarragon and sauté for about 1 minute. Pour in the wine and cream and boil until the sauce is thick enough to coat a spoon, about 3 minutes. Season the sauce to taste with salt and pepper.

To serve, arrange the salmon fillets on top of the beds of spinach and top with the cream sauce.

SALMON PATTIES
8 SERVINGS

These are great served with tiny new potatoes and a green vegetable like sugar snap peas, but they also make wonderful burgers on buns with tomatoes, lettuce and mayonnaise.

- 5 tablespoons olive oil, plus more if needed
- 1 cup chopped shallots, or red onion
- 1 cup dry white wine
- ½ cup freshly squeezed lemon juice
- ¼ cup capers, drained, rinsed and chopped
- 2 pounds skinless, bonelesss salmon, cut into 1-inch pieces
- 3 cups fresh bread crumbs, made from fresh homemade-style or French bread, crusts removed
- 2 large eggs, lightly beaten
- 2 tablespoons chopped fresh dill
- 1½ teaspoons salt
- Freshly ground black pepper

In a heavy frying pan over moderate heat, heat 3 tablespoons of the olive oil. Add the shallots or red onion and sauté them until they are soft but not brown, about 5 minutes. Raise the heat to moderately high and add the white wine, lemon juice and capers. Cook the mixture, stirring frequently, until almost all liquid has evaporated, about 15 minutes. Transfer the mixture to a large bowl and refrigerate it for at least 1 hour.

In a food processor, pulse the salmon until it is coarsely ground. (Do not over-process.) Alternatively, chop the salmon to a coarse grind with a sharp knife. Add the ground salmon to the shallot mixture. Stir in the bread crumbs, lightly beaten eggs, dill, salt and a very generous grinding of black pepper.

Divide the mixture equally into 8 portions and, using your hands, shape each portion into a compact patty about ¾-inch thick. Transfer the patties to a baking sheet, cover them with plastic wrap and refrigerate them until ready to cook. (The patties may be made up to 8 hours ahead of time.)

In a large heavy frying pan over moderately high heat, heat the remaining 2 tablespoons of olive oil. Working in batches, add the salmon patties to the frying pan and sauté them until they are golden brown and cooked through, about 3 minutes per side. Add a little more oil to the pan if needed. As the patties are cooked, transfer them to a platter and keep them warm in a low oven while you cook the remainder.

SALMON SOUFFLÉ
4 SERVINGS

- 4 tablespoons unsalted butter, softened
- 2 tablespoons freshly grated parmesan cheese
- 3 tablespoons all-purpose flour
- 1 cup milk, heated
- ½ teaspoon salt
- ¼ teaspoon ground white pepper
- 4 egg yolks
- 6 egg whites
- 1½ cups cooked salmon, separated into small flakes
- ½ cup grated Swiss cheese

This is an excellent way to use leftover cooked salmon, but you may use drained canned salmon. Remember to rush this impressive soufflé to the table the minute it is ready; otherwise it will deflate.

Preheat the oven to 400°F.

Coat the bottom and sides of a 2-quart soufflé dish with 1 tablespoon of the butter. Sprinkle in the parmesan cheese and tip the dish to spread the cheese as evenly as possible over the bottom and sides.

In a large non-reactive saucepan, melt the remaining 3 tablespoons of butter over moderate heat. When the foam begins to subside, add the flour and, stirring constantly with a wire whisk, cook the mixture for about 2 minutes. Do not let it brown. Remove the butter and flour mixture from the heat and pour in the heated milk all at once, whisking vigorously to incorporate it. Return the saucepan to high heat and continue whisking until the sauce comes to a boil and is thick and smooth. Add the salt and pepper. Remove the saucepan from the heat and whisk in the egg yolks, one at a time, whisking well after each addition. Set the mixture aside.

In a large mixing bowl, beat the egg whites with an electric beater or a balloon whisk until they are stiff enough to form unwavering peaks. Stir a large spoonful of beaten egg white into the waiting sauce to lighten it. Stir in the salmon and the grated Swiss cheese. Using a rubber spatula and an over-and-under cutting motion, gently, but thoroughly, fold in the remaining egg white. Spoon the soufflé mixture into the prepared dish and smooth the top.

Place the soufflé in the middle of the oven and immediately reduce the temperature to 375°F. Bake the soufflé for about 35 minutes, or until it is puffed and golden brown. Serve it immediately, directly from the dish.

MOCK COULIBIAC
6 SERVINGS

A true coulibiac is made with brioche dough. This version uses frozen puff pastry for an easier, but still very impressive, main course.

- 4 cups court bouillon (see recipe index)
- 1½ pounds salmon, preferably thick centre cut
- 6 tablespoons unsalted butter, melted
- ¼ cup finely chopped shallots or red onion
- ¼ pound mushrooms, finely chopped
- 2 teaspoons chopped fresh tarragon leaves, or ½ teaspoon dried tarragon
- Salt
- Freshly ground black pepper
- ¾-pound package frozen puff pastry, thawed
- 1 cup cooked wild rice
- 3 hard-boiled eggs, shelled and cut in half
- 1¼ cups commercial sour cream
- Fresh dill sprigs for garnish

Bring the *court bouillon* to a simmer in a large non-reactive saucepan. Add the salmon and poach it for about 6 minutes, or just until it turns opaque. Drain the salmon and let it cool. Remove all the skin and bones and flake it into large pieces. Place it in a dish and pour 4 tablespoons of the melted butter over it, tossing gently to coat. Cover and refrigerate the salmon until needed.

In a large heavy frying pan, add the shallots and mushrooms to the remaining melted butter and sauté them over moderate heat, stirring occasionally, for 20 minutes or until they are very soft. Remove the pan from the heat and stir the mushroom mixture into the cooked wild rice. Stir in the tarragon and salt and pepper to taste. Set the rice mixture aside.

Preheat the oven to 425°F. On a lightly floured surface roll out ¾ of the pastry into a rectangle about 14 inches long and 12 inches wide. Place the rectangle on a lightly greased baking sheet. Spread half the rice mixture down the length of the pastry, leaving about 4 inches at the ends and sides. Cover the rice with the salmon. Lay the egg halves end to end over the salmon and dollop them evenly with ¼ cup of the sour cream. Spoon the remaining rice evenly over the top. Bring the dough up around the sides of the filling to enclose it completely. Roll out the remaining pastry and cut it into decorative shapes. Brush the undersides with water and arrange the shapes on the *coulibiac*. Bake the *coulibiac* for 25 minutes or until puffed and brown.

Remove the *coulibiac* to a platter and garnish it with sprigs of dill. To serve, cut it into thick slices and pass the remaining sour cream in a bowl.

SMOKED SALMON - CUCUMBER TRIANGLES
12 HORS D'OEUVRES

- 12 thin slices dark rye bread
- ½ pound thinly sliced smoked salmon
- 1 large English cucumber (sometimes called seedless cucumber)
- 4 ounces whipped cream cheese
- Sweet mustard, such as honey mustard
- Small sprigs of dill for garnish

Smoked salmon, cucumber and cream cheese are always popular as a team, but this hors d'oeuvre is of a different stripe. The geometric presentation never fails to intrigue and the taste is cool and delightful.

I make these frequently and even have what I think of as my smoked salmon hors d'oeuvre plate, a very large cut-glass plate that shows off these little appetizers beautifully.

Trim the crusts from the bread and cut each slice to make a 2½-inch equilateral triangle. (I use a template cut from cardboard.) Discard the bread trimmings (or save them for another use) and cover the bread while you make the topping.

Cut the salmon into ½-inch wide strips. Peel the cucumber and cut it in half lengthwise. Using a small spoon, scoop out and discard the seeds. Using a very sharp knife, cut the cucumber lengthwise into very thin strips. Trim the strips so they are ½ inch wide.

Spread the bread triangles with cream cheese. Arrange alternating bands of salmon and cucumber over the cheese, trimming them to fit the shape. (I find scissors more useful than a knife for this.)

Place the *hors d'oeuvres* on a large plate or platter, arranging them attractively. The *hors d'oeuvres* may be made up to this point an hour or so ahead of time. Cover them with plastic wrap and refrigerate.

Just before serving, top each *hors d'oeuvre* with a small dab of mustard and garnish with a sprig of dill.

Smoked Salmon and Goat Cheese Tart
4 to 6 Servings

- Enough pastry for a 9-inch pie crust (your own favourite pastry recipe or frozen pastry dough), rolled out and placed in a well-buttered deep pie plate (preferably glass or ceramic)
- 1 tablespoon butter
- ½ cup finely chopped leeks
- 3 large eggs plus one egg yolk
- About 1 cup light cream or whole milk, or a mixture of both
- 4 ounces goat cheese, crumbled
- 4 to 6 ounces smoked salmon, cut into thin slivers
- ½ teaspoon finely chopped fresh dill, or ¼ teaspoon dried dill
- 1 teaspoon prepared Dijon mustard

Served with a green salad, this tart makes a lovely brunch or luncheon entrée. I find the recipe makes just the right amount of filling for my 9-inch pie plate.

Preheat the oven to 375°F. Prepare the pastry in the pie plate and refrigerate it until ready to bake.

Melt the butter over low heat and cook the leeks in it, stirring occasionally, for about 10 minutes or until they are very soft but not browned.

While the leeks are cooking, break 1 egg into a measuring cup and add enough of the cream or milk to reach the ½-cup level. Pour this mixture into a medium-sized bowl. Repeat the procedure with the other two whole eggs and cream or milk, and then add 1 egg yolk to the bowl. Whisk the mixture together lightly with a fork. Add the goat cheese, smoked salmon, dill and mustard and whisk again just until all the ingredients are incorporated.

Spread the leeks evenly over the bottom of the prepared pie shell. Pour the egg mixture into the shell to within ¼ inch of the rim. Bake the tart for 30 to 35 minutes in the preheated oven or until it is puffed and golden. Let it rest for at least 20 minutes before cutting it into wedges to serve.

SMOKED SALMON SALAD
4 SERVINGS

- 3 tablespoons balsamic vinegar
- ½ teaspoon prepared Dijon mustard
- 6 tablespoons extra-virgin olive oil
- Salt
- Freshly ground black pepper
- 6 cups mesclun (baby salad greens)
- 6 ounces thinly sliced smoked salmon
- 1½ tablespoons drained capers
- ½ small red onion, thinly sliced
- 20 ripe red cherry tomatoes, halved
- 4 hard-cooked eggs, peeled and quartered

If tiny grape tomatoes are available, substitute them for the cherry tomatoes but use twice the number and leave them whole. Asparagus spears or artichoke hearts may also be added to this colourful and refreshing salad.

Pumpernickel bread served on the side is a nice addition and makes this a light but filling luncheon.

In a small bowl, whisk together the balsamic vinegar and Dijon mustard. In a slow stream, whisk in the olive oil to blend well. Season the dressing with salt and freshly ground pepper to taste.

Place the salad greens in a large bowl. Toss them with enough dressing to coat them lightly. Divide the greens among 4 large chilled plates. Arrange the smoked salmon slices over the greens on each plate, dividing them equally. Drizzle a little more dressing over the salmon. Sprinkle the salmon equally with the capers. Garnish the salads with equal amounts of the red onion, tomatoes and hard-cooked egg quarters.

Capelin & Smelts

Towards the end of June when I was growing up, we'd wait with anticipation to hear the cry, "the capelin are in." Then we'd head to the beach equipped with buckets. There, ankle deep in capelin, we'd scoop up as many as we could of the thousands of wriggling silvery fish that had come on shore to spawn. Newfoundlanders call it the "capelin scull", and children and adults alike participate in gathering this annual ocean bounty.

Capelin, often spelled "caplin", are *mallotus villosus*, a small schooling fish and a close relative to smelts. They are found in cold deep waters on offshore banks all around Newfoundland and southern Labrador and move inshore in masses only at spawning time. Besides being salted by Newfoundlanders for their own consumption, capelin were often used as bait for the cod fishery or spread on gardens as fertilizer. Now there is a commercial fishery for capelin, mainly providing the roe to oriental markets.

Capelin are important as a species, providing a vital link in the food chain. Their decline is of great concern to the cod fishery because capelin are the cod's main food. They also provide a major source of food for Atlantic salmon and a host of other fish, sea birds and marine animals.

The meat of the capelin is particularly delicious and high in nutrition. Like most oily fish, the quality of fresh capelin deteriorates rapidly so it is best to cook them as soon as possible. Dried salted capelin may be kept almost indefinitely if tightly wrapped and stored in a cool dry place.

Fresh capelin are wonderful grilled, roasted, pan-fried or deep-fried. Dried capelin are a favourite Newfoundland meal at a picnic or "boil-up". They are traditionally roasted on a stick over an open fire and eaten with thick slices of homemade bread.

American smelts, *osmerus mordax*, sometimes called rainbow smelt, are also found in waters all around Newfoundland and southern Labrador. They are similar to capelin in size, texture and flavour.

Capelin and smelts are often cooked whole and can be easily boned after cooking by merely opening up the belly cavity and lifting out the bones and tail all in one piece.

GRILLED CAPELIN
4 TO 6 APPETIZER SERVINGS

- 12 fresh capelin
- Lemon wedges (optional)
- Mustard of choice (optional)

Prepare a barbecue for moderately high heat and set the grill about 4 inches above the coals.

Rinse and dry the capelin, but leave them whole. (The heads and bones will pull off easily after they are cooked.)

Arrange the capelin on one face of a large, flat, double-sided grill. If the grill is not large enough for all the capelin to fit side by side, alternated with heads and tails in opposite directions, cook them in 2 batches. There should be enough space between the capelin for the heat to circulate for even cooking. Clamp the grill shut and place it on the barbecue.

Grill the capelin for about 10 to 12 minutes per side, turning several times, or until the capelin are almost charred.

Remove the capelin from the barbecue, open up the grill and invite guests to help themselves to the capelin, accompanied, if they wish, with a squeeze of lemon or a little mustard.

The capelin must be very fresh and grilled just as they come from the ocean, not skinned, boned or even gutted. They should be eaten outdoors, straight from the barbecue grill. No seasoning is necessary, but you might wish to provide lemon wedges or a small bowl of piquant mustard.

Have handy a stack of paper napkins, a receptacle in which to throw the capelin carcasses and discarded napkins, and a communal finger bowl (a large bowl of lukewarm water with thin slices of floating lemon).

A 12- to 16-inch square, flat, double-sided hinged grill makes the cooking much easier and prevents the slippery capelin from falling through the regular barbecue grill. (These grills or "camp toasters" are inexpensive and are available at many hardware stores and kitchen shops.)

When the capelin are done, each diner pinches off the heads and tails and lifts off and eats the fillets from both sides of the capelin, discarding the bones and guts.

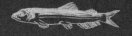

Pan-Fried Stuffed Capelin

4 Servings

The "stuffing" in this recipe is really just a seasoned butter that melts into the capelin as they cook.

- 2½ pounds capelin
- Coarse salt
- ¼ cup unsalted butter, softened
- 1 teaspoon finely chopped fresh dill, or ½ teaspoon dried dill
- 1 tablespoon finely chopped fresh parsley
- 2 eggs
- ½ cup milk
- ½ cup rye flour
- ¾ cup fine dry bread crumbs
- About ½ cup vegetable oil
- Lemon wedges

Clean the capelin by splitting them the full length of the belly. Remove the fins, heads, tails and bones without cutting through the back of the fish. Sprinkle the capelin generously with coarse salt and set them aside at room temperature for about 40 minutes.

Meanwhile, in a small bowl, cream together the butter, dill and parsley until well combined.

In a shallow bowl, beat the eggs lightly with a fork. Stir together the rye flour and breadcrumbs and spread the mixture on a piece of waxed paper.

Rinse the capelin and dry them thoroughly. Put a small pat of the herbed butter in the cavity of each capelin and press the sides together well. Dip each capelin in egg. Then roll them in the crumb mixture. Arrange the capelin in one layer on a wire rack set over a baking sheet. Refrigerate the fish for at least 30 minutes to firm up the coating.

In a large heavy frying pan, heat 3 tablespoons of vegetable oil over moderately high heat until it is very hot, but not smoking. Working in small batches of 3 to 4 capelin, add them to the oil. Fry the capelin, turning them once or twice, until they are golden brown and crisp. Transfer the capelin to a heated platter and keep them warm in a low oven. Repeat the procedure with the remaining capelin, adding more vegetable oil as necessary. Serve the capelin as soon as they are all fried. Garnish them with the lemon wedges.

DEEP-FRIED CAPELIN
4 SERVINGS

Deep-fried whole capelin are always a popular treat. Homemade bread is the traditional accompaniment.

- 3 pounds whole capelin
- White vinegar
- 3 eggs
- ½ cup milk
- 2 tablespoons olive oil
- 1½ teaspoons salt
- Freshly ground black pepper
- ½ cup all-purpose flour
- 1 cup fine dry bread crumbs
- Vegetable oil for deep frying
- Lemon wedges

Rinse the capelin, but leave them whole. (The heads and bones will pull off easily after they are cooked.)

In a large shallow glass or ceramic baking dish, arrange the capelin side by side. Pour the vinegar over them to cover and allow them to marinate at room temperature for 15 minutes. Drain the capelin and pat them dry. Discard the vinegar.

In a large bowl, beat the eggs together with the milk, olive oil, salt and a generous grinding of black pepper. Place the flour on a large piece of waxed paper and the bread crumbs on another large piece of waxed paper.

Pour the vegetable oil into a deep heavy saucepan or deep fryer. Heat the oil to 375°F on a deep-frying thermometer. Working in small batches of 3 to 4 capelin, dust the fish lightly with flour, shaking off the excess, dip them into the egg mixture, turning them to coat, and then roll them in the bread crumbs. Carefully add the first batch of capelin to the oil. Fry the capelin, turning them once or twice, until they are golden brown and crisp. Using tongs, transfer the capelin to paper towels to drain and keep them warm in a low oven. Repeat the procedure with the remaining capelin, making sure the oil returns to 375°F between each batch.

Serve the capelin as soon as they are all fried. Garnish them with the lemon wedges.

BAKED SMELTS WITH OLIVES AND SAVORY
4 SERVINGS

- 6 tablespoons unsalted butter
- ¼ cup drained, pitted and slivered brine-packed black olives
- 2 pounds smelts, cleaned but with heads and tails left on
- Salt
- ¼ cup olive oil
- 1 tablespoon dried summer savory
- Freshly ground black pepper
- 2 tablespoons freshly squeezed lemon juice
- 2 tablespoons finely chopped parsley

Summer savory is Newfoundland's most popular herb. It grows well here and is dried for use in a large variety of recipes. Don't substitute the powdered stuff found in jars in the spice section of the supermarket; it's usually winter savory, which has a very different taste. If you can't obtain Newfoundland savory, look for savory marked as the summer variety.

Preheat the oven to 425ºF.

In a large heavy frying pan, melt 4 tablespoons of the butter over low heat until it becomes a light amber colour. Do not let it burn. Stir in the olives. Remove the frying pan from the heat and set it aside.

Dry the smelts well and lightly salt the inside of each cavity.

In a shallow flameproof baking dish large enough to hold the smelts in one layer, heat the remaining 2 tablespoons of butter and the olive oil over moderate heat until the mixture begins to sizzle. Stir in the savory and a generous grinding of black pepper. Roll the smelts around in the herbed fat until they are evenly coated on both sides. Place the dish in the hot oven and bake, basting the fish with the hot fat every 5 minutes or so, for 20 to 25 minutes, or until the fish are brown and firm to the touch. Carefully transfer the smelts to a heated platter, arranging them attractively in rows.

Gently reheat the olive and savory sauce, stir in the lemon juice and parsley and pour the sauce evenly over the smelts.

PICKLED FRIED SMELTS
6 TO 8 SERVINGS

- 3 pounds smelts
- 1½ cups white vinegar
- ¼ cup unsalted butter, softened
- ¼ cup finely minced parsley
- 3 to 4 tablespoons olive oil
- 1 cup sugar
- 1 teaspoon whole black peppercorns
- 1 clove garlic, coarsely chopped
- 1 small onion, sliced into thin rings

This dish is served cold, usually as part of a composed salad that includes other pickled foods, such as beets or pickled eggs. Mustard and homemade bread are traditional accompaniments.

After they are fried and pickled, the smelts will keep well for about a week in the refrigerator.

Clean the smelts by splitting them the full length of the belly. Remove the fins, heads, tails and bones without cutting through the back of the fish. Place the smelts in a shallow non-reactive dish and pour the vinegar over them. Let the smelts marinate in the vinegar at room temperature for about 15 minutes, turning them gently once or twice.

Meanwhile, in a small bowl, cream together the butter and parsley until well combined.

Remove the smelts from the marinade, but do not discard the vinegar. Wipe the smelts dry and spread them open, skin side down, on a large piece of waxed paper. Spread the flesh sides of the smelts evenly with the parsley butter. Refold the fish around the butter.

In a large heavy frying pan, heat 3 tablespoons of olive oil over moderately high heat until it is very hot, but not smoking. Working in batches of 4 to 5 smelts, fry them until they are golden brown on both sides. If necessary, add a little more oil to the pan between batches. As they are fried, transfer the fish to a large shallow non-reactive dish, keeping them in one layer if possible.

In a large non-reactive saucepan, combine the reserved vinegar, sugar, peppercorns, garlic and onion. Bring the mixture to a boil, stirring to dissolve the sugar. Pour the hot pickle mixture evenly over the fried smelts. Cover the dish and refrigerate the smelts for at least 18 hours before serving.

CLAMS

For centuries, even before Europeans settled in Newfoundland and Labrador and only aboriginal peoples fished from its shores, clams have been harvested for food.

The term "clam" is used to denote a broad range of bivalve molluscs found along the coast of Newfoundland and Labrador. The leading commercial species are the Stimpson surf clam, *spisula polynyma*, sometimes called bar clam, and the soft-shell clam, *mya arenaria*. The surf clam is a deep-water species found mainly off the southern part of the island. The soft-shell clam is found in sandy bays and estuaries all around Newfoundland and Labrador.

Clams are filter feeders and burrow themselves into the sediment with a tongue-shaped organ, usually referred to as a "foot". The posterior end of the clam has a siphon with great extendibility, usually referred to as the clam's "neck". A clam cannot close its shell tightly if its neck extends beyond the edges of its shell.

The surf clam is larger than the soft-shell clam and can reach a diameter of about nine inches. Its shell is heavy. Soft-shell clams have thin, brittle shells that are chalky coloured. The average harvest size of soft-shell clams is two to three inches, although they can grow to about seven inches.

When you buy live clams, make sure they are actually alive. The shell should be tightly closed or, if gaping slightly, should close when tapped. The neck of a soft-shell clam should contract when touched. Discard any clams with broken shells.

Clams kept covered with damp paper towels in the refrigerator will stay alive for up to a week after harvest or for several days after purchase. Never store them in water, on ice or in an airtight container. They will die. If you dig your own clams, let them stand for several hours in sea water to purge them of sand. Don't use fresh water.

All clams have a sweet light flavour and are extremely versatile. They may be baked, fried, steamed or used in chowders and pasta dishes.

NEWFOUNDLAND CLAM CHOWDER

6 SERVINGS

- 3 cups shucked hard-shelled clams, chopped, 1½ cups liquor reserved, or substitute 3 cups canned clams, liquor from the cans reserved
- 6 ounces salt pork fat, rind removed, cut into ¼-inch dice
- 1½ cups finely chopped onions
- 6 small boiling potatoes, cut into ½-inch dice
- 2 cups water
- ½ teaspoon dried summer savory
- 1 bay leaf
- 2 cups milk, heated
- 1 cup heavy cream
- Salt
- Freshly ground black pepper

Traditionalists insist that clam chowder improves if, after cooking, it is allowed to rest off the heat, but not refrigerated, for at least an hour before serving to allow the flavours to mingle. If you choose to do this, reheat the chowder very gently while stirring. It should not be allowed to come anywhere near a boil.

If using hard-shelled clams, such as surf clams or bar clams, simmer them in their own liquor in a small saucepan, covered, for about 30 minutes. This step is not necessary for canned clams.

In a large heavy saucepan, sauté the salt pork over moderately high heat, stirring, until it is golden and has rendered all its fat. Using a slotted spoon, transfer the salt pork to paper towels to drain. Pour off and discard all but 2 tablespoons of the fat in the pan.

In the fat remaining in the pan, cook the onion over moderately low heat, stirring occasionally, until it is soft but not brown, about 5 minutes. Stir in the potatoes and the water.

Cover and simmer the mixture for 10 minutes or until the potatoes are barely tender. Stir in the clams, reserved liquor, savory and bay leaf. Simmer the mixture, uncovered, for 5 minutes. Stir in the heated milk and the cream. Heat gently and simmer for a few minutes longer. Do not let the chowder boil. Taste and season the chowder with salt, if necessary, and plenty of freshly ground black pepper. Discard the bay leaf.

Serve the chowder from a heated tureen or in heated soup bowls. The reserved salt-pork dice may be discarded or a teaspoon or so may be sprinkled over each serving.

Creamy Clam Dip
About 2 Cups

- 8 ounces cream cheese, softened
- ¼ cup sour cream
- 2 6½-ounce cans minced clams, drained, reserving 3 table-spoons juice
- ¼ cup finely chopped red bell pepper
- 1 small red onion, minced
- 2 tablespoons minced fresh parsley leaves
- 1 teaspoon Worcestershire sauce
- 1 tablespoon freshly squeezed lemon juice
- Small pinch cayenne
- Salt

The popularity of dips as a cocktail accompaniment is well-established and this one is always a favourite. I like to keep a few cans of clams in the cupboard so, if unexpected guests drop by, I can whip up this tasty dip in a matter of minutes. Serve it with crisp crackers, melba toast or wedges of pita bread.

In a medium-sized bowl, whisk the cream cheese and sour cream together until smooth. Stir in the clams, pepper, onion, parsley, Worcestershire sauce, lemon juice and cayenne. If the dip seems too thick, thin it with a tablespoon or more of the reserved clam juice. Taste and add salt if necessary.

GRILLED CLAMS WITH SALSA AND BACON
48 HORS D'OEUVRES

- ¼ cup finely chopped shallots or red onion
- 1½ cups diced, seeded tomatoes
- 1 small jalapeño pepper, seeded and finely chopped
- 1 clove garlic, minced
- 3 tablespoons freshly squeezed lemon juice
- 1 tablespoon finely chopped fresh basil
- 1 tablespoon finely chopped fresh parsley
- 1 tablespoon finely chopped fresh cilantro (or substitute mint)
- Salt and freshly ground black pepper
- ¼ pound sliced bacon
- About 6 cups coarse salt
- 4 dozen clams in their shells, scrubbed

A bed of rock salt helps keep the cooked clams in place on the platter. A little of the salt will stick to the shells, adding extra flavour to these delightfully lively little appetizers.

In a medium-sized bowl, combine the shallots or onion, tomatoes, jalapeño pepper and garlic. Stir in the lemon juice. Add the basil, parsley and cilantro and stir to combine well. Season to taste with salt and pepper. Refrigerate the salsa, covered, for at least 2 hours to allow the flavours to blend.

In a large frying pan over moderate heat, cook the bacon slices, turning occasionally, until they are crisp. Transfer the bacon to paper towels to drain and cool. Crumble the bacon and set it aside.

Prepare a barbecue for moderately high heat. Cover the bottom of 2 platters with a ¼-inch-thick layer of coarse salt.

Arrange the clams directly on the barbecue rack. Cover and grill until the clams open, turning occasionally, about 8 minutes. Discard any clams that do not open. Remove the clams from the barbecue rack.

Using potholders to protect your hands, twist off and discard the top shells of the clams. Arrange the clams, shell side down, on top of the salt on the platters. Spoon some salsa on top of each clam. Sprinkle with the reserved bacon and serve while hot.

Steamed Clams

4 Servings

*Provide plenty of napkins and a large
bowl for the discarded clam shells.*

- 8 dozen soft-shell clams
- 3 tablespoons unsalted butter
- 1 small onion, finely chopped
- 1 garlic clove, minced
- 2 tablespoons minced fresh parsley leaves
- 2 tablespoons freshly squeezed lemon juice
- ½ teaspoon salt
- ¾ cup melted unsalted butter

Have ready 8 small heated bowls or ramekins and 1 very large heated bowl.

Scrub the clams under cold running water. Discard any with broken shells and those whose necks (siphons) do not retract when prodded.

In an 8- to 10-quart heavy pot equipped with a cover, melt the 3 tablespoons of butter over moderately low heat. Add the onions and garlic and cook, stirring frequently, for about 5 minutes or until they are soft but not brown. Stir in the parsley. Add 3 cups of water and bring the mixture to a boil over high heat. Add the clams, cover the pot, and steam for 7 to 8 minutes, or until the clams are opened.

With a large slotted spoon, transfer the clams to the large heated bowl. Discard any clams that remain unopened. Strain the broth remaining in the pot through a sieve lined with a double thickness of dampened cheesecloth into a bowl.

Divide the broth equally among 4 of the small bowls or ramekins. Stir the lemon juice and salt into the melted butter and divide it equally among the other 4 small bowls or ramekins. Arrange a bowl of broth and a bowl of lemon butter at each table setting.

To eat the steamed clams, remove each clam from its shell with a small fork. Dip it into the broth to moisten it (this will also remove any traces of sand). Then dip it into the hot lemon butter.

LINGUINE WITH CLAMS

6 SERVINGS

- ¼ cup extra-virgin olive oil
- ½ pound thinly sliced pancetta (unsmoked Italian bacon), cut into thin strips, or substitute regular bacon
- 1 clove garlic, thinly sliced
- 2 pounds clams in their shells, scrubbed
- 1 cup bottled clam juice
- ½ cup dry white wine
- ½ teaspoon dried hot red pepper flakes
- 1 pound dried linguine
- ¼ cup chopped fresh parsley

For this pasta dish, I recommend using a sturdy dried pasta rather than fresh or egg linguine. The fresh pasta will absorb too much of the sauce. You will note that there is no accompanying cheese in this recipe. That's because, for some reason or other, it does not marry well with the combination of ingredients here.

In a large heavy frying pan, heat 2 tablespoons of the oil over moderately high heat until hot, but not smoking. Sauté the *pancetta*, stirring occasionally, until it is golden and crisp, about 6 minutes. Add the garlic and sauté, stirring, about 30 seconds longer.

Stir in the clams, clam juice, wine and pepper flakes and boil, covered, until the clams open, about 4 to 5 minutes. (Discard any clams that do not open after 5 minutes.)

While the clams are cooking, cook the pasta in a 6-quart pot of well-salted boiling water until just firm to the bite. Drain the pasta in a colander and return it to the pot. Add the clam mixture and simmer, stirring, 30 seconds.

Stir in the parsley and the remaining oil. Divide the mixture among 6 heated deep plates and serve immediately.

COD COUSINS

A number of relatives of cod are found at varying depths of water around Newfoundland and Labrador. All are lean and flavourful with whitish tender meat. With a few exceptions, they may be used interchangeably or substituted in any recipe calling for cod or for lean white fish.

Haddock, *melanogrammus aeglefinus*, belong to the same family as cod. Once much more abundant, their stocks, like cod, have been greatly reduced, but they are still found all around the coast of Newfoundland.

Haddock are a dark purplish-gray on the head and back. The lateral line is black, but lightens below to silver with a slight tinge of pink. Fish in the commercial catch are generally between two and five pounds.

Haddock are usually marketed as fresh and frozen fillets. They may often be found split and smoked as "finnan haddies'. Haddock may be substituted for cod in most recipes.

Hake are also related to cod. Several varieties of hake are present in Newfoundland waters, but the commercial catch is limited to the red hake, *urophycis cuss*, and the white hake, *urophycis tenuis*. Both are fished off the south coast of the island and are normally two to six pounds in weight.

Hake are cod-like, but have only two, rather than three, dorsal fins. No commercial differentiation is made among the species of hake, but they vary considerably in colour. The back may be grey to reddish to muddy brown and the belly white, grey or yellowish.

In some cases hake may be substituted for cod or haddock, but I don't recommend it for chowders because it becomes soft and tends to fall apart.

Pollock, *pollachius virens*, are also members of the cod family. Caught all around Newfoundland and southern Labrador, they are eagerly sought as a commercial species.

Pollock differs from cod and haddock by having a pointed snout and projecting lower jaw. The back is brownish-green, paling to a yellowish- or greenish-grey on the sides. The belly is silvery. Fish in the commercial catch are usually from about two to eight pounds in weight.

Pollock are usually marketed as frozen "Boston bluefish" fillets. This fish is extremely versatile. Most frozen breaded fish or fish sticks are made from pollock and it is the main ingredient in artificial crabmeat.

SMOKED HADDOCK KEDGEREE
4 SERVINGS

- 6 cups water
- 2 teaspoons salt
- 1 cup long-grained rice
- 3 tablespoons butter
- 2 cups flaked smoked haddock, bones removed
- 2 teaspoons curry powder
- ¼ cup milk
- 1 tablespoon finely chopped parsley
- 4 hard-cooked eggs, coarsely chopped

Kedgeree is derived from an Indian dish called Khicharhi and the recipe was probably brought to Newfoundland from England. Originally a breakfast dish, it is now more often served for lunch or supper.

In a large pot, bring the water to a boil over high heat. Add the salt and pour in the rice in a slow, thin stream so that the water continues to boil. Reduce the heat to moderate and cook the rice, uncovered, for about 18 minutes, or until it is tender but still fairly firm to the bite. Drain the rice thoroughly.

In a heavy 10- to 12-inch frying pan, melt the butter over moderate heat. When the foam begins to subside, add the rice, smoked haddock and curry powder. Stirring constantly, cook the mixture for 2 or 3 minutes. With the back of a spoon, flatten the mixture and spread it evenly to the sides of the pan. Pour the milk over the top, cover, and reduce the heat to low. Cook the mixture for about 5 minutes or until the milk is absorbed.

Stir in the parsley and chopped egg and taste for seasoning. Fluff the kedgeree with a fork and transfer it to a serving dish or individual plates.

Haddock with Horseradish Butter
4 Servings

- ¼ cup unsalted butter, softened
- 1 tablespoon prepared horseradish
- 2 tablespoons freshly squeezed lime juice
- 1 teaspoon Worcestershire sauce
- 1 tablespoon finely minced parsley
- 2 tablespoons vegetable oil
- 1½ pounds haddock fillets, cut into 4 equal-sized pieces
- Salt
- Freshly ground black pepper
- 1 teaspoon grated lime zest

Boiled new potatoes go well with the haddock. Any leftover horseradish butter may be frozen for future use and is good with other fish or shellfish.

In a medium sized bowl, stir together the butter, horseradish, lime juice and Worcestershire sauce. With a hand-held electric mixer, beat the ingredients together until very light and fluffy. Stir in the parsley. (The horseradish butter may be made ahead of time and refrigerated, covered.)

Season the haddock fillets on both sides with salt and freshly ground black pepper.

In a large heavy frying pan, heat the oil over moderate heat. Add the haddock fillets and, regulating the heat so the fillets do not scorch, fry them for 4 to 6 minutes on each side (depending on their thickness), turning them carefully with a wide spatula. The fillets are done when they flake easily when prodded gently with a fork.

To serve, transfer the fillets to 4 heated plates. Place a dollop of the horseradish butter on each fillet and sprinkle with a little of the lime zest.

CURRIED HADDOCK
4 SERVINGS

Rice is the usual complement to curried foods, but I sometimes serve sweet potatoes with this dish. Their flavour blends nicely with the light spices here.

- 2 tablespoons liquid honey
- 2 tablespoons prepared Dijon mustard
- 1½ teaspoons curry powder
- ½ teaspoon ground cumin
- ¼ teaspoon ground coriander
- 1 teaspoon dried thyme
- ½ teaspoon salt
- 1½ pounds 1-inch thick haddock fillets, cut into large chunks
- 2 tablespoons unsalted butter
- ¾ cup prepared mango chutney, heated

In a large ceramic or glass bowl, mix together the honey, mustard, curry, cumin, coriander, thyme and salt, combining the ingredients well. Add the fish pieces and toss to coat them. Cover the bowl and refrigerate the fish for at least 2 hours and up to 6 hours.

In a large heavy frying pan, melt the butter over moderate heat. Add the fish pieces in batches (do not crowd the pan) and, turning frequently, cook the fish until just cooked through, about 8 minutes. As each batch is cooked, transfer it to a platter and keep it warm in a low oven.

When all the haddock is cooked, divide it equally among 4 heated dinner plates and spoon some of the hot chutney alongside each serving.

STEAMED WHOLE HAKE ORIENTAL-STYLE

4 SERVINGS

- 1 whole fresh hake, about 2 pounds, cleaned, with head removed but skin and tail left on
- 1 tablespoon salt
- 1 tablespoon finely minced fresh ginger root
- 3 tablespoons soy sauce
- 3 tablespoons water
- 1 tablespoon white sugar
- 2 green onions, cut crosswise into 1½-inch pieces and shredded lengthwise with a sharp knife
- 2 tablespoons vegetable oil
- 1 tablespoon Asian sesame oil
- Sprigs of fresh cilantro or parsley

This is a wonderful way to experience the flavour of fresh hake or any other small whole white-fleshed fish. When brought to the table, the fish should still be sizzling.

Choose a roasting pan large enough to accommodate the whole hake, and one that can be fitted with a rack and a heat-proof platter.

Rub the fish inside and out with the salt. Rinse it well with cold water and pat it dry. Sprinkle the cavity with half the minced ginger. Place the fish on a platter that will fit into the roasting pan on a rack. Sprinkle the fish with the remaining ginger. Place the platter on the rack in the roasting pan.

Pour boiling water into the pan to reach to just below the rack. Place the pan across 2 burners on the stove and turn the heat to high on both. Bring the water to a boil again, reduce the heat to moderately low, cover the pan and cook the fish for 12 minutes. Test for doneness by inserting a fork into the head section of flesh. It should flake easily.

Meanwhile, in a small non-reactive saucepan, combine the soy sauce with the water and sugar. Bring the mixture to a boil, stirring until the sugar is dissolved. Boil the mixture for 1 minute longer. Keep the mixture warm over low heat.

In another small saucepan, heat the vegetable oil and sesame oil until almost, but not quite, smoking.

Remove the platter with the fish from the pan. Pour off any liquid that may have accumulated on the platter. Drizzle the fish with the heated soy-sauce mixture. Sprinkle it evenly with the shredded green onions. Then pour the hot oil over the fish and serve immediately, garnished with the cilantro or parsley.

HAKE CASSEROLE

4 SERVINGS

This recipe makes good use of leftover hake, but is so rich and delicious that you might want to cook a fillet of fish especially for it.

- 4 tablespoons unsalted butter, softened
- 1 tablespoon finely minced onion
- ¼ pound fresh mushrooms, thinly sliced
- 1 small green pepper, finely chopped
- 2 tablespoons flour
- 1½ cups whole milk or light cream, heated
- 1½ cups cooked hake, flaked
- 1 cup coarse bread crumbs, made from day-old homemade-type white bread
- ¾ teaspoon salt
- Freshly ground black pepper
- 2 tablespoons medium-dry sherry
- 2 tablespoons unsalted butter, melted

Preheat the oven to 375°F. Coat the bottom and sides of a 1½-quart shallow baking dish with 1 tablespoon of the softened butter.

In a heavy saucepan, melt the remaining 3 tablespoons of butter over moderate heat. Add the onion, mushroom and green pepper and cook, stirring frequently, until the vegetables are soft but not brown. Stir in the flour and blend for 1 or 2 minutes or until it is well incorporated. Remove the saucepan from the heat and pour in the heated milk or cream all at once, whisking all the ingredients together. Return the saucepan to moderate heat and, whisking constantly, cook until the mixture comes to a boil and is quite thick.

Remove the saucepan from the heat and stir in the flaked hake, half the bread crumbs, salt, a generous grinding of black pepper and the sherry. Taste and adjust seasonings.

Pour the mixture into the prepared baking dish and spread the remaining bread crumbs over the top. Drizzle the melted butter as evenly as possible over all. Bake the casserole for about 30 minutes or until nicely browned. Serve directly from the baking dish.

STUFFED POLLOCK TURBANS
6 SERVINGS

Traditionally made with cod, these easy-to-make turbans are also good with pollock. Mashed potatoes and a green vegetable are the usual accompaniments.

- 2 cups bread crumbs, made from day-old homemade-type white bread
- 2 tablespoons finely grated onion
- ½ teaspoon salt
- ¼ teaspoon freshly ground black pepper
- 1 teaspoon dried summer savory
- 2 tablespoons unsalted butter, softened
- 6 skinless 6- to 8-ounce pollock fillets, neatly trimmed
- ½ cup unsalted butter, melted
- Parsley sprigs for garnish

Preheat the oven to 375°F.

In a medium-sized bowl, mix together the bread crumbs, onion, salt, pepper and savory.

Using a pastry brush or paper towel, coat the insides of 6 large muffin tins or ramekins evenly with the 2 tablespoons of softened butter. Dry the pollock fillets well and carefully coil one inside each tin or ramekin, pressing them firmly against the sides. Fill the centers with the stuffing mixture, dividing it equally.

Drizzle the melted butter evenly over the top of each turban. Cover the muffin tins or ramekins loosely with a sheet of aluminum foil. Bake them for 20 minutes. With the aid of a spatula, carefully remove the turbans and transfer them to heated plates. Garnish each turban with a sprig of parsley.

POLLOCK WITH BROWN BUTTER AND CAPERS

4 SERVINGS

The browned butter adds a nut-like flavour to the pollock. Rice or noodles complement this recipe nicely.

- 3 tablespoons unsalted butter
- ¼ cup minced shallots or red onion
- 1 tablespoon freshly squeezed lemon juice
- ¼ cup minced fresh parsley leaves
- 2 tablespoons drained bottled capers, minced
- 1 tablespoon finely chopped lemon pulp
- 2 teaspoons freshly grated lemon zest
- 4 6- to 8-ounce pollock fillets
- Salt
- Freshly ground black pepper
- Lemon wedges or slices for garnish

Preheat the oven to 350°F.

In a small frying pan, melt the butter over moderate heat until it just begins to brown and stir in the shallot or red onion. Cook the vegetables until they are soft, about 2 minutes. Remove the frying pan from the heat and stir in the lemon juice.

In a small bowl, stir together the parsley, capers, lemon pulp and lemon zest.

Place the fish fillets on a lightly oiled shallow baking pan. Sprinkle them with salt and pepper. Brush the fillets with the butter mixture and sprinkle with the parsley mixture. Bake the fillets in the middle of the oven until they are just cooked through, about 12 minutes. Garnish them with lemon wedges or slices.

CRAB

Just a few days after I moved back to Newfoundland from Ontario, my Aunt Daphne brought me a most welcome gift, a heap of exquisitely tasty cooked snow crab legs, specifying that I need not share them with anyone. She knows how much I love crab.

The snow crab, *chionoecetes opilio*, also known as queen crab, is found in waters all around Newfoundland and southern Labrador and is an extremely valuable resource. Crabs are caught in baited cages, or pots, that are dropped to sandy bottoms anywhere from depths of three feet to over 1,000 feet. The average commercial weight of a snow crab is from one to two pounds.

The snow crab has a body that is almost circular and four pairs of flattened walking legs plus a pair of powerful claws. The shell is a mottled light brown on the back and creamy coloured on the underside. The male is larger than the female and it is usually only the male that reaches the legal catch size.

When cooked, the shell of the snow crab turns bright pinkish-orange. On the surface, the meat is also a pinkish-orange colour, but is snowy white inside. Crabmeat is made up of fine tender filaments, but it has a firm texture. The flavour is sweet and rich.

When buying live crabs, select the most active ones and store them, wrapped in dampened newspaper, in the refrigerator, where they should stay alive for 12 hours or more. Live crabs are usually steamed in the same manner as lobsters (by dropping them headfirst into salted boiling water and cooking them for about 15 minutes per pound). Steamed crab is delicious served simply with melted butter, but the cooked meat may be used in any recipe for crab.

When using canned or frozen crabmeat, remember that the meat has already been cooked and needs only to be heated through. It should always be picked over to remove bits of shell and cartilage. It can be used in appetizers, salads, soups and a variety of other wonderful dishes.

CRAB SOUP WITH SHERRY
4 TO 6 SERVINGS

- 3 tablespoons unsalted butter
- 3 tablespoons all-purpose flour
- 3 cups basic fish stock, or shellfish stock (see recipe index), brought to a simmer
- 1 cup milk
- 2 cups fresh cooked crabmeat or canned or frozen crabmeat, thawed
- ½ cup medium-dry sherry
- 1 cup heavy cream
- Salt
- White pepper
- Drops freshly squeezed lemon juice
- 2 tablespoons finely chopped fresh chives

My friend Helen introduced me to this wonderful recipe many years ago. Because the soup is so rich, it is best served as a luncheon main course, with perhaps a leafy salad and some fresh fruit to finish.

In a large heavy saucepan, melt the butter over moderate heat. When the foam begins to subside, add the flour, reduce the heat to low and, whisking constantly, cook the mixture for 1 or 2 minutes. Do not let it brown. Remove the saucepan from the heat and pour in the simmering stock all at once. Stir in the milk. Return the saucepan to high heat and, whisking constantly, bring it to a boil. Continue to boil, whisking, for 1 or 2 minutes or until the mixture is thick and smooth.

Add the crabmeat and sherry. Reduce the heat to low, partially cover the pot and, stirring occasionally, cook the mixture for 10 minutes. Add the cream and heat gently for a few minutes longer. Add salt, white pepper and a few drops of lemon juice to taste.

Serve the soup in heated soup bowls and sprinkle each serving with chopped chives.

CHILLED CRAB SOUP
4 SERVINGS

- 2 cups torn romaine lettuce leaves, tightly packed
- 1 tablespoon coarsely chopped fresh cilantro leaves
- 2 cups coarsely chopped peeled and seeded cucumbers
- ½ cup coarsely chopped green bell pepper
- ¼ cup coarsely chopped onion
- 1 garlic clove, chopped
- 3 tablespoons extra-virgin olive oil
- 2 tablespoons red wine vinegar
- 1 cup cubed, crustless white bread, preferably from a French-style loaf
- 1½ cups cold water
- 1 tablespoon freshly squeezed lime juice
- 1 teaspoon salt
- 1 cup cooked crabmeat, fresh or frozen, thawed
- 2 tablespoons minced fresh chives

This delightfully green herbaceous soup sings of summer and lunch on the patio. It needs no cooking and is a great way to stretch a small amount of crabmeat.

In a food processor fitted with a steel blade, purée 1½ cups of the romaine lettuce leaves, the cilantro leaves, chopped cucumbers, green bell peppers, onion and garlic until very finely chopped. Add 2 tablespoons of the olive oil and the vinegar and pulse until the mixture is fairly smooth. Add the bread, stirring it in with a small spatula, and let it stand for about 5 minutes, to allow the bread to absorb moisture from the other ingredients. Then pulse again until very smooth.

Transfer the contents of the food processor to a large bowl. Stir in the water, lime juice and salt. Cover the bowl and refrigerate the soup for at least 2 hours and up to 6 hours.

Just before serving, finely shred the remaining ½ cup of romaine lettuce with a sharp knife.

Taste the soup for seasoning and add more salt if necessary. (Salt loses savour when chilled.)

Divide the soup among 4 chilled bowls. Place a mound of the shredded romaine lettuce in the centre of each serving. Divide the crabmeat equally and mound it on top of the lettuce. Sprinkle the chives over the top and drizzle each serving with about ½ teaspoon of olive oil.

CRABMEAT SUSHI ROLLS
ABOUT 3 DOZEN PIECES

Many people think sushi means raw fish, but it actually refers to the Japanese "rice sandwich" which can be made with cooked or raw fish.

- 1 cup raw white short-grain Japanese-style sticky rice, or "sushi" rice (available in oriental markets and many supermarkets)
- About 3 tablespoons seasoned rice vinegar
- ½ large English cucumber (sometimes called seedless cucumber)
- 1 large ripe avocado
- 2 tablespoons freshly squeezed lemon juice
- 4 8- by 7-inch pieces of toasted nori (dried toasted laver seaweed, available in oriental markets)
- 6 ounces cooked crab leg meat, thawed if frozen, picked over
- Wasabi (Japanese green horseradish, available in oriental markets)
- Soy sauce
- Pickled ginger (available in oriental markets and some supermarkets)

Cook the rice according to the package directions. Transfer the rice, while still hot, to a large shallow bowl. Sprinkle the rice with as much of the vinegar as necessary to moisten it lightly, tossing it carefully. Cover the seasoned rice with a dampened cloth and keep it at room temperature until ready to use (no more than 2 hours).

Peel the cucumber and cut it in half lengthwise. Using a small spoon, scoop out the seeds and discard them. Then cut the cucumber lengthwise into ¼-inch strips. Peel and pit the avocado. Cut it into ¼-inch-thick strips. Place the lemon juice in a small shallow bowl. Add the avocado strips and toss them about with a spoon to coat them with the lemon juice.

Working with one sheet of *nori* at a time, and with a long side facing you, spread about ¾ cup of the rice in an even layer on each sheet, leaving a ½-inch border on the long sides. Arrange ¼ of the avocado strips horizontally across the middle of the rice and arrange ¼ of the cucumber strips and ¼ of the crabmeat on top of the avocado. Dab the crabmeat with a small amount of the *wasabi*. Beginning with a long side, roll up the *nori* tightly jelly-roll fashion. Repeat the procedure for the remaining sheets of *nori*. As each roll is assembled, wrap it tightly in plastic wrap and refrigerate it. Chill the rolls for at least 1 hour and up to 6 hours.

When ready to serve, cut each roll with a sharp knife into ¾-inch-thick slices and lay the slices side by side on a platter. Serve the *sushi* rolls with small bowls of soy sauce, additional *wasabi* and pickled ginger.

CRAB GRATIN
4 FIRST-COURSE SERVINGS

- 2 tablespoons minced carrot
- 2 tablespoons minced celery
- 2 tablespoons minced red bell pepper
- 1 tablespoon unsalted butter
- ½ cup basic fish stock (see recipe index) or substitute chicken broth
- ¼ cup dry white wine
- ¼ teaspoon dried tarragon, crumbled
- ½ cup heavy cream
- ½ pound fresh lump crabmeat, picked over (about 1½ cups)
- Freshly squeezed lemon juice to taste
- Salt
- Freshly ground pepper
- ¼ cup freshly grated parmesan cheese
- Lightly toasted thin French bread slices

The first time I tasted this fabulous gratin, my friend Meredith brought it to a potluck supper. It disappeared in no time and the next day we were all clamouring for the recipe.

Preheat the broiler.

In a small heavy saucepan cook the carrot, celery and bell pepper in the butter over moderate heat, stirring, for about 5 minutes, or until the vegetables are soft but not brown. Add the stock or broth, wine and tarragon and boil the mixture until the liquid has almost completely evaporated. Add the cream and boil the sauce, whisking, until it is thickened, 1 to 2 minutes. Stir in the crabmeat, lemon juice and salt and pepper to taste.

Divide the mixture among four ½-cup shallow baking dishes (or for a more impressive presentation, use scallop shells). Sprinkle the cheese over the crab mixture and set the dishes in a shallow baking pan. Broil the *gratins* about 4 inches from the heat for about 2 minutes or until they are bubbling and golden. Serve the *gratins* with the toast.

CRABMEAT CURRY
6 SERVINGS

Although this fragrant curry incorporates Indian ingredients, most are available in any supermarket. Choose basmati rice or jasmine rice for their fine authentic flavour.

- 2 small dried hot red chili peppers
- 2 tablespoons vegetable oil
- 1 medium onion, coarsely chopped
- 3 large garlic cloves, minced
- 1-inch piece fresh ginger root, grated
- 1 teaspoon black mustard seeds
- ½ teaspoon black peppercorns
- 1½ teaspoons ground cumin
- 1 teaspoon ground coriander seeds
- ½ teaspoon turmeric
- 1½ pounds lump crabmeat
- ¼ cup packed fresh cilantro leaves
- 1½ cups canned unsweetened coconut milk
- 1½ teaspoons salt or to taste
- Cooked rice
- 3 green onions with some of their tops, thinly sliced

Wearing rubber gloves, chop the hot peppers into 1-inch pieces and reserve, along with any seeds.

In a large saucepan, heat the oil over moderately high heat until hot but not smoking, and cook the mustard seeds until they begin to pop. Stir in the onion, garlic, ginger root, reserved hot peppers with seeds, and peppercorns and cook, stirring constantly, until the hot peppers are just browned, 3 to 4 minutes. Stir in the other spices until combined well. Add the crabmeat and cook the mixture, gently stirring occasionally (avoid breaking up the crab) for about 5 minutes.

While the crab mixture is cooking, chop the cilantro. Stir it into the crab mixture with the coconut milk and salt and simmer until slightly thickened, 6 to 8 minutes. Taste the curry and adjust the seasonings.

Spoon the curry over the cooked rice and garnish with the green onions.

CRAB CAKES
4 SERVINGS

These crab cakes are made with lots of crabmeat and not much filler, so they require gentle handling.

- 3 tablespoons vegetable oil
- 1 red bell pepper, cut into ¼-inch dice
- 1 yellow bell pepper, cut into ¼-inch dice
- 6 slices firm white sandwich bread, crusts discarded
- 1 pound lump crabmeat, picked over
- 2 tablespoons chopped fresh cilantro
- ¼ cup mayonnaise
- 2 tablespoons Old Bay seasoning (available in specialty shops and some supermarkets)
- 1 fresh jalapeño pepper, seeded and chopped fine (wear rubber gloves)
- 1 tablespoon minced garlic
- Freshly ground black pepper
- Salt
- Tartar sauce and/or cocktail sauce (see recipe index)

In a large frying pan, heat 1 tablespoon of the vegetable oil over moderately high heat until hot but not smoking and sauté the bell pepper until it begins to soften. Let the pepper cool. In a food processor, pulse the bread into fine crumbs. In a large bowl, stir together the bell pepper, crabmeat, cilantro, mayonnaise, Old Bay seasoning, jalapeño, garlic, 2 tablespoons of the bread crumbs, a generous grinding of black pepper and salt to taste. Combine the mixture well and chill it for at least 45 minutes.

With a ¼-cup measure, scoop the crab mixture into 8 portions and pat each into ¾-inch-thick disk. Spread the remaining bread crumbs on a sheet of waxed paper and gently press each crab cake into them, turning it to coat the cake evenly. To help prevent crumbling during cooking, chill the crab cakes, covered loosely, for at least 1 hour.

Preheat the oven to 250°F.

In a large frying pan, heat 1 tablespoon of the vegetable oil over moderately high heat until very hot and sauté half the crab cakes until golden brown, about 5 minutes per side, turning the cakes carefully. As the crab cakes are done, transfer them to a platter and keep them warm in a low oven. Add the remaining tablespoon of oil to the frying pan and sauté the remaining crab cakes in same manner, transferring them to the oven as they are cooked.

Serve the crab cakes with tartar sauce and/or cocktail sauce.

CRAB TART
6 SERVINGS

Served with a green salad, crab tart
makes a wonderful luncheon.

- Pastry dough for a 10-inch pie shell
- 3 tablespoons unsalted butter
- 1 medium-sized onion, finely chopped
- 1 medium-sized yellow bell pepper, finely chopped
- 2 stalks celery, finely chopped
- ½ cup mayonnaise
- 1 tablespoon Worcestershire sauce
- ¾ cup fine fresh bread crumbs
- ¼ teaspoon cayenne pepper
- ¾ pound lump crabmeat, picked over
- 1 7-ounce jar roasted red peppers, drained and finely chopped
- ¼ cup chopped fresh parsley leaves
- 4 green onions, including some of the green tops, thinly sliced

On a lightly floured surface, roll out the dough to a thin 13-inch round and fit it into a 10-inch round tart pan. Trim the dough flush with the rim and press it to the sides of the pan. With a fork, prick the bottom and sides of the pie shell all over. Chill the pie shell in the refrigerator for at least 30 minutes.

Preheat the oven to 375°F. Line the pie shell with buttered aluminum foil and fill it with pie weights, dried beans or raw rice. Bake the pie shell in the middle of the oven for 20 minutes. Carefully remove the foil and weights. Return the pie shell to the oven and bake it until it is a pale golden brown, about 10 minutes longer. Remove the pie shell from the oven and place it on a wire rack to cool. Increase the oven temperature to 425°F.

In a heavy frying pan, melt the butter over moderately low heat. Add the onion, yellow pepper, and celery and cook, stirring, until the vegetables are soft but not brown.

In a large bowl, whisk together the mayonnaise and Worcestershire sauce. Stir in ½ cup of the bread crumbs and the cayenne pepper. Stir the crabmeat into the mayonnaise mixture along with the softened vegetables and the butter remaining in the frying pan. Add the chopped roasted peppers, parsley and green onions and stir to combine the ingredients well. Taste and adjust the seasonings.

Spoon the filling into the pie shell. Smooth the top and sprinkle it with the remaining ¼ cup bread crumbs. Bake the tart in the middle of the oven for 20 to 25 minutes, or until the top begins to brown.

Let the tart cool for about 15 minutes before serving.

Flatfish

Flatfish are just that. Their bodies are flat and they swim on one side. They don't start out that way, however. They begin life swimming in an upright position and, like most other fish, have an eye on either side of their heads. But before long, one eye starts to move around to the other side. At first, the fish swims in a lopsided manner. Eventually, it begins to swim on its side, both eyes facing upward. Some species become right-eyed; others have eyes on the left.

The flatfish found in waters around Newfoundland and Labrador include American plaice (*hippoglossoides platessoides*), Atlantic halibut (*hippoglossus hippoglossus*), Greenland halibut (*reinhardtius hippoglossoides*), known to most Newfoundlanders as turbot, and varieties of flounder, such as winter flounder (*pseudopleuronectus americanus*), witch flounder (*glyptocephalus cynoglossus*) and yellowtail flounder (*limanda ferruginea*).

Flatfish are groundfish, so-called because they generally dwell and feed near the bottom of the ocean. Most are caught with trawl nets, but some are landed with gill nets in the inshore fishery.

Delicate texture and flavour characterize the meat of all flatfish. Most are best with the skin removed. Flatfish may be grilled, baked, poached or steamed and they adapt well to many sauces.

Some varieties of flatfish, particularly flounder, are marketed as "sole". The true sole, however, is a European fish found in waters from Denmark to the Mediterranean. Flounder is more delicate and is generally not suited to recipes calling for Dover sole.

All of the following recipes may be used interchangeably, but since the size of the fillets differs with the species, allow about one-half pound per person.

FISH ROLLS WITH DRESSING
6 SERVINGS

This is a very old Newfoundland recipe. A century ago, lemons were rarely available, so cooks used vinegar instead of lemon juice. For those who didn't keep cows, rendered pork fat would have replaced the butter.

- 2 cups soft bread crumbs, made from homemade-type white bread
- 1 small onion, finely chopped
- 2 teaspoons dried summer savory
- ¼ teaspoon salt
- Freshly ground black pepper
- 4 tablespoons butter, melted
- 2 tablespoons hot water
- 6 skinless flounder fillets, approximately the same size, about 2 pounds total
- 2 tablespoons freshly squeezed lemon juice

Preheat the oven to 425°F. Lightly grease a large shallow baking dish.

In a bowl, combine the bread crumbs, chopped onion, savory, salt and a generous grinding of black pepper. Stir in 2 tablespoons of the melted butter and the 2 tablespoons of hot water and stir to combine the mixture well.

Dry the fish fillets and lay them side by side on a clean work surface or a large piece of waxed paper. Using a large spoon, divide the bread-crumb mixture evenly among them, spreading it over the fillets. Beginning at the narrow end, roll up each fillet jelly-roll fashion. Secure each roll with a wooden cocktail pick. Place the rolls side by side in the prepared dish.

Combine the remaining 2 tablespoons of melted butter with the lemon juice and pour it evenly over the fish rolls. Bake the rolls for 20 minutes.

To serve, transfer the fish rolls to a heated platter or individual plates.

FLOUNDER WITH ORANGE
4 SERVINGS

Fish is often cooked or served with lemon, but other citrus fruits make for a delicious change of pace.

- 3 tablespoon unsalted butter
- 4 skinless, boneless flounder fillets, about 6 ounces each
- ¼ cup finely chopped shallots or red onion
- ¼ cup finely chopped celery
- 1 cup soft fresh bread crumbs, from white home-style bread
- 1 large orange, peeled, all white pith removed, seeded and diced
- ½ teaspoon salt
- ¼ teaspoon freshly ground black pepper
- ¼ cup freshly squeezed orange juice

Preheat the oven to 425°F. Using a pastry brush or paper towel, coat the inside of a baking dish large enough to hold the fish fillets in one layer evenly with 1 tablespoon of the butter. Dry the flounder fillets well and place them side by side in the dish.

In a large heavy frying pan, melt the remaining 2 tablespoons of butter over moderately low heat. When the foam subsides, add the shallots or onions and the celery and cook them, stirring occasionally, for 6 or 7 minutes or until they are soft but not brown. Remove the pan from the heat and add the bread crumbs, diced orange, salt, pepper and orange juice. Toss the mixture together lightly and spread it evenly over the fish. Bake the fish for about 20 minutes or until the topping turns golden brown and the fish flakes easily when prodded with a fork.

FLOUNDER WITH PINE NUTS
4 SERVINGS

- ¼ cup pine nuts
- ¼ cup unsalted butter
- 1 tablespoon minced fresh chives
- 4 6-ounce flounder fillets
- Salt
- Freshly ground black pepper
- ½ cup all-purpose flour on a plate
- Lemon wedges
- Sprigs of parsley

I love pine nuts with just about anything and they provide a satisfying crunchy contrast to tender fish. This dish takes only minutes to prepare. I like to serve it over a bed of hot fluffy rice.

In a large non-stick frying pan, sauté the pine nuts in 2 tablespoons of the butter over moderately high heat, stirring frequently, until golden. Add the chives. Remove the frying pan from the heat and, using a slotted spoon, transfer the pine nuts and chives to a dish.

Season the flounder fillets with salt and pepper and dredge them in the flour, shaking off the excess. In the frying pan, heat the remaining butter over moderately high heat until the foam subsides and sauté the flounder until it just flakes, about 2 minutes on each side. Transfer the fish to 4 heated plates and spoon the pine nut mixture evenly over each fillet. Garnish each serving with lemon wedges.

QUENELLES WITH GINGER-TOMATO SAUCE
4 SERVINGS

- ¼ cup minced onion
- 1 tablespoon olive oil
- 1 teaspoon grated fresh ginger
- A 14- to 16-ounce can of tomatoes with their juice, finely chopped
- Salt
- Freshly ground black pepper
- 1¼ pounds chilled halibut or winter flounder fillets
- 1 egg, chilled
- ½ teaspoon salt
- ½ cup chilled heavy cream
- Up to ½ cup fine bread crumbs made from homemade-type white bread
- Parsley sprigs for garnish

Quenelles are often made with pike, a freshwater fish with excellent flavour but so webbed with tiny bones that a quenelle mixture, made by pushing a purée through a fine sieve to eliminate the bones, is the most convenient way of eating it. This recipe, using boneless halibut or flounder, eliminates the need for a sieve, but the resulting delicate quenelles are every bit as delicious. To be most successful, the ingredients should be cold.

In a frying pan, cook the onion in the olive oil over low heat, stirring frequently, until it is softened. Add the ginger and cook the mixture for about 2 minutes longer. Add the tomatoes with their juice and simmer the sauce, stirring occasionally, for about 10 minutes or until it is reduced and thickened. Season the sauce to taste with salt and pepper and keep it warm.

In a food processor, preferably fitted with a plastic blade, purée the fish with the egg and ½ teaspoon of salt. With the motor running, add the cream in a thin stream and blend the mixture until it is just smooth.

In a large wide saucepan, bring 2 inches of lightly salted water to a simmer. To make a test for consistency, scoop out and form an oval mound of the fish mixture with 2 dessert spoons dipped in cold water, dropping the mound into the simmering water. It should hold its shape. If it is too loose and disintegrates, pulse in enough bread crumbs by tablespoons until the mixture holds its shape well. Once the right consistency has been achieved, form the rest of the *quenelles* in the same manner and poach them at a bare simmer, turning them occasionally, for about 6 minutes, or until they are springy to the touch and roll over easily. Transfer the *quenelles* with a slotted spoon to paper towels to drain briefly and divide them among 4 heated plates. Spoon the sauce over and around the *quenelles* and garnish them with sprigs of parsley.

BLACKENED HALIBUT
4 SERVINGS

Blackened fish—fish coated with spices and seared quickly in a hot pan—has become a favourite method for sealing in lots of flavour.

- 1 tablespoon sweet paprika
- 1 teaspoon dried oregano
- 1 teaspoon dried thyme
- ¼ teaspoon cayenne or to taste
- 1 teaspoon sugar
- 1 teaspoon salt
- ½ teaspoon freshly ground black pepper
- 4 halibut fillets (about 2 pounds)
- 2 large garlic cloves, thinly sliced
- 2 tablespoons olive oil
- 2 tablespoons unsalted butter
- Lemon wedges

In a small bowl, combine the paprika, oregano, thyme, cayenne, sugar, salt and black pepper. Pat the halibut fillets dry and sprinkle the spice mixture on both sides of the fillets, coating them well and rubbing in the spices with your fingertips.

In a large frying pan, preferably cast iron, sauté the garlic in the oil over moderate heat, stirring frequently, until it is golden brown. Discard the garlic. (It is used only for flavouring.) Add the butter and heat it until the foam subsides. In the fat, sauté the halibut for about 4 minutes on each side, or until it is cooked through. Transfer the fillets with a slotted spatula to heated plates and serve them with the lemon wedges.

Lettuce-Wrapped Halibut Packages
4 Servings

- ¼ cup unsalted butter, softened
- 1 large lemon
- 3 tablespoons finely chopped shallots
- Salt and freshly ground black pepper
- 12 unblemished large outer romaine lettuce leaves (from 2 heads)
- 4 6- to 8-ounce halibut fillets, cut thick

Almost since the beginning of time, fruit and vegetable leaves have been used to seal in the moisture and flavour of cooked foods. There are no exotic ingredients here, but the result is wonderful.

Preheat the oven to 450°F.

Coat the inside of a 13- by 9-inch glass or ceramic baking dish with 1 tablespoon of the butter. Cut 4 very thin slices from the lemon and reserve them. Squeeze and reserve the juice from the remaining lemon.

In a small bowl, mash together the remaining butter, 1 teaspoon of the lemon juice and the shallots. Season the mixture with salt and pepper to taste. Sprinkle any remaining lemon juice over the bottom of the baking dish.

In a large pot of lightly salted boiling water, cook the romaine lettuce leaves for 1 minute. Immediately transfer them with tongs to a large bowl of ice water to cool. Drain the lettuce leaves, but do not dry them. (The water clinging to the leaves will make it easier to wrap the packages.) Cut the tough ribs from the lettuce leaves, but leave at least 1 inch of the top of the leaves intact.

Place one lettuce leaf on a work surface. Place another leaf on the first leaf, overlapping them to cover any holes. Season one halibut fillet with salt and pepper and place it crosswise in the centre of the lettuce. Spread the top of the fish with ¼ of the shallot butter. Place another leaf over the top and wrap up the bottom leaves to form a neat package. Transfer the package to the baking dish. Make 3 more packages in the same manner, arranging them close together in the baking dish.

Top each package with a lemon slice. Cover the packages with a sheet of waxed paper or parchment paper. Then tightly cover the dish with aluminum foil.

Bake the packages in the middle of the oven for about 20 minutes, or until they feel firm to the touch. Serve the lettuce-wrapped halibut with the juices in the bottom of the baking dish poured over the packages.

OVEN-FRIED HALIBUT
4 SERVINGS

- ¼ cup bottled capers, rinsed
- 2 pounds halibut fillets, cut 1 inch thick
- 1½ teaspoons salt
- ½ teaspoon freshly ground black pepper
- 2 small lemons, thinly sliced crosswise
- ¼ cup finely chopped flat-leaf parsley, or, if unavailable, substitute curly parsley
- 1 cup extra-virgin olive oil

You can have this highly flavoured dish on the table in less than an hour. I like to serve it with small whole new potatoes cooked in their skins, spooning a little of the flavoured oil from the cooked fish over the potatoes.

Preheat the oven to 325°F.

Chop the capers coarsely. Pat the fish dry. Sprinkle the fish evenly with the salt and pepper and let it stand 10 minutes at room temperature. Arrange half the lemon slices in a single layer in an 8-inch square glass or porcelain baking dish. Arrange the fish in a single layer over the lemon. Top the fish with the capers, the remaining lemon slices and 3 tablespoons of parsley. Pour the oil evenly over the fish. Bake the halibut in the middle of the oven, uncovered, until the fish just flakes and is cooked through, about 30 minutes.

Serve the fish with some of the lemon slices, capers and olive oil spooned over the top. Garnish each serving with a sprinkle of the remaining parsley.

HALIBUT WITH GREEN SAUCE
4 SERVINGS

In this uncomplicated recipe the halibut is seared quickly in a frying pan, then topped with a piquant lemon-caper sauce.

- 1 teaspoon finely grated lemon zest
- ¼ cup freshly squeezed lemon juice
- 1 tablespoon drained capers
- ½ teaspoon minced garlic
- Salt and freshly ground black pepper
- 6 tablespoons extra-virgin olive oil
- ¼ cup finely chopped parsley
- 4 ½-inch-thick halibut steaks with skin, about 2 pounds total
- Lemon wedges

In a small bowl, whisk together the lemon zest, lemon juice, capers, garlic, and salt and pepper to taste. Add 4 tablespoons of the oil in a slow stream, whisking constantly until blended. Whisk in the parsley.

Pat the halibut dry and season it with salt and pepper. In a large non-stick frying pan, heat the remaining 2 tablespoons of oil over moderate heat until hot but not smoking. Cook the halibut, turning the steaks once, until they are golden brown on both sides and just cooked through, about 7 minutes total.

Serve the halibut topped with the sauce and garnished with lemon wedges.

BAKED TURBOT ROLLS
6 SERVINGS

Serve this with rice or pasta and you'll have an elegant and flavourful, yet simple, entrée.

- 6 slices lean bacon, finely chopped
- ¼ cup finely chopped shallots or red onion
- 1 small green bell pepper, finely chopped
- ½ cup dry white wine
- 1 28-ounce can diced tomatoes, including juice
- 1 tablespoon finely chopped fresh basil, or 1 teaspoon dried basil
- Salt
- Freshly ground black pepper
- 6 8-ounce skinless turbot fillets, cut in half lengthwise
- ¼ cup ripe black olives, pitted and finely chopped
- ¾ cup fine bread crumbs, made from fresh homemade-style bread
- 2 tablespoons finely chopped fresh parsley leaves
- 2 tablespoons olive oil

Preheat the oven to 400°F.

In a large heavy frying pan over moderate heat, cook the bacon until it is crisp. Transfer the bacon to paper towels to drain and discard all but 2 tablespoons of the fat. In the fat remaining in the frying pan, cook the shallots or red onion and the bell pepper over moderately low heat, stirring, for about 5 minutes, or until they soften. Stir in the wine and boil the mixture to a boil. Boil for 1 or 2 minutes, scraping up any brown bits that cling to the pan. Add the tomatoes with their juice, the basil and salt and pepper to taste. Simmer the sauce, stirring occasionally, for 10 minutes, or until it is thickened.

Arrange the turbot fillets on a work surface and sprinkle them evenly with the finely chopped black olives. Beginning at the narrow end, roll up each fillet half jelly-roll fashion.

Secure each roll with a wooden toothpick.

In a shallow oiled baking pan, about 15 by 10 by 2 inches, arrange the fish rolls, seam sides down and not touching each other. Pour the sauce evenly over them and bake the rolls for 10 minutes.

Meanwhile, in a bowl, stir together the bread crumbs, parsley, drained bacon and salt and pepper to taste. Sprinkle the mixture on top of the fish rolls and drizzle the olive oil evenly over the top. Continue to bake the rolls for another 10 minutes, or until the fish flakes easily when prodded with a fork.

To serve, transfer 2 rolls to each of 6 heated plates. Spoon some of the sauce and topping over each serving.

TURBOT WITH VEGETABLE SAUCE
4 SERVINGS

Mashed potatoes are perfect with this impressive dish.

- ¼ cup finely chopped shallots, or red onion
- ¼ cup white wine vinegar
- ¼ cup dry white wine
- ½ cup light cream, or half and half
- 3 tablespoons olive oil
- 1 pound mushrooms, thinly sliced
- 2 medium-sized zucchini, trimmed but not peeled, cut into julienne (matchstick-sized pieces)
- Salt
- Freshly ground black pepper
- 4 8-ounce turbot fillets, about ¾ inch thick
- ¼ cup cold butter, cut into small pieces
- 2 medium-sized tomatoes, peeled, seeded and diced (about 1 cup)
- ½ cup loosely packed chopped fresh spinach leaves

In a small heavy saucepan, combine the shallots or red onion with the vinegar. Over high heat, boil the mixture, stirring occasionally, until most of the liquid evaporates, about 5 minutes. Add the wine and boil to reduce the mixture to about 2 tablespoons. Whisk in the cream or half and half and set the sauce aside.

Preheat the oven to 400°F.

In a large heavy frying pan, heat 2 tablespoons of the olive oil over moderately high heat. Add the mushrooms and sauté them, stirring frequently, until they are fully cooked and a deep golden brown. Add the zucchini and sauté, tossing, for about 2 minutes longer. Season the mixture to taste with salt and freshly ground pepper and set it aside, loosely covered.

Lightly oil a large baking sheet. Place the turbot fillets on the sheet and brush them with the remaining 1 tablespoon of olive oil. Bake until the fish is just cooked through and opaque in the centre, about 10 minutes.

Meanwhile, bring the cream sauce to a simmer. Reduce the heat and add the cold butter, a few pieces at a time, whisking until it is incorporated. Remove the sauce from the heat and add the tomatoes and spinach, stirring gently until the spinach just wilts. Season the sauce to taste with salt and freshly ground pepper.

To serve, place a turbot fillet on each of 4 heated plates. Arrange the mushroom-zucchini mixture around the fish. Spoon the sauce over the fish.

Baked Turbot with Lemon-Dill Sauce

6 Servings

The sauce here is rich, so the turbot is best served with plainly cooked vegetables such as boiled potatoes and steamed green beans.

- 6 8-ounce turbot fillets, about ¾ inch thick
- 2 tablespoons vegetable oil
- ¾ cup Vermouth, or dry white wine
- ¼ cup finely chopped red onion
- 1 tablespoon freshly squeezed lemon juice
- ½ cup chilled unsalted butter, cut into small bits
- 1 tablespoon finely chopped fresh dill, or 1 teaspoon dried dill
- Salt
- Freshly ground pepper, preferably white

Preheat the oven to 400°F.

Use a little of the vegetable oil to lightly grease a large baking sheet. Place the turbot fillets on the sheet and brush them with the remaining oil. Bake the fish until it is just cooked through and opaque in the centre, about 10 to 12 minutes.

Meanwhile, in a small heavy non-reactive saucepan over high heat, bring the Vermouth or white wine, red onions and lemon juice to a boil. Continue to boil rapidly, uncovered, until the mixture is reduced to ¼ cup, about 7 minutes. Reduce the heat to low. Add the butter, 1 or 2 bits at a time, whisking until each addition has melted into the sauce before adding more. Remove the pan from the heat and stir in the dill. Season to taste with salt and white pepper.

Divide the turbot fillets among 6 heated plates. Pour the sauce over and around the fillets and serve at once.

HERRING

From my kitchen window overlooking Random Sound, I sometimes see a large congregation of seagulls above a small patch of water. It probably means they are following a school of herring, one of their favourite foods.

A herring school is a shimmering, greenish-glinting mass of fish that moves slowly along in a circular pattern. Herring spend their lives feeding on plankton and small sea creatures that they filter through their toothless mouths. In turn, they are eaten by birds, seals and other mammals, including people.

A herring is an elongated, streamlined fish with a body much deeper than it is thick. It is bluish-green along the back with silver sides and belly. The herring's scales are large, loosely attached and cover the entire body of the fish.

Atlantic herring, *clupea harengus harengus*, are found in relatively shallow water all around Newfoundland and Labrador and have always been an important part of the commercial fishery. They are generally caught using gillnets or purse-seine nets and are most often processed quickly in fish plants for food or bait. Commercially caught herring weigh between about one-third and one and one-half pounds.

Unless you happen to be around when herring boats come in, fresh herring are not often available because there is no longer a great demand for them. However, frozen herring, salted herring, marinated herring, kippers and sardines, which are very young herring, are readily available in delicatessens and most supermarkets.

Herring are oily fish with distinctively soft meat and a large number of bones. In fresh herring recipes it is best to use fillets no longer than about four inches and cook them at a high temperature, making any small bones soft and edible. Regardless of the cooking method, the backbone should always be removed. When it is lifted out, many of the smaller bones will come with it.

Fresh or frozen herring, thawed, are best when pan-fried or baked. Preserved herring, such as smoked and pickled fillets, may be used in salads, casseroles and a great number of other tasty preparations. Salted herring should be soaked in water or milk before cooking.

Herring and Beet Salad

6 Servings

There's scarcely a Newfoundland woman I know who doesn't pickle beets in early autumn. Here they add contrasting colour and texture to a composed herring salad.

- ½ cup mayonnaise
- ¼ cup sour cream
- ¼ cup olive oil
- ¼ cup white-wine vinegar
- Salt
- Freshly ground black pepper
- 12 small new potatoes, about 2 inches in diameter, washed but not peeled
- 2 green apples, such as Granny Smiths, peeled, cored and cut into ½-inch dice
- ¼ cup small pickled white onions, coarsely chopped
- Romaine lettuce leaves
- 1 12-ounce jar wine-marinated herring, drained and cut into bite-sized pieces
- 2 cups sliced pickled beets, drained and diced
- 3 hard-boiled eggs, shelled and sliced

In a small bowl, whisk together the mayonnaise, sour cream, olive oil and vinegar. Season the dressing to taste with salt and black pepper.

Place the potatoes in large heavy saucepan. Add cold water to cover. Bring the potatoes to a boil, cover and continue to boil until they are just tender, about 15 minutes. Drain the potatoes and cool them completely. Cut the potatoes into ½-inch dice.

In a large bowl, toss together the potatoes, apples and pickled onions. Add just enough of the dressing to coat and toss well.

Line a platter with the lettuce leaves. Mound the potato-and-apple salad in the centre of the platter. Arrange the herring pieces, beets and eggs attractively around the salad. Pass the remaining dressing separately in a small bowl.

Mustard-Sauced Herring with Potatoes

4 Servings

- 2 pounds small boiling potatoes, scrubbed, but not peeled
- 1½ pounds fresh herring fillets
- 1 tablespoon freshly squeezed lemon juice
- ½ teaspoon salt
- 6 tablespoons unsalted butter, softened
- 1 cup finely chopped onions
- 2 tablespoons prepared Dijon mustard

Whether the herring is fresh, salted, pickled or smoked, mustard is always a welcome complement.

Preheat the oven to 350°F.

Drop the potatoes into enough boiling salted water to cover them completely and boil them briskly, uncovered, for about 20 minutes, or until they show no resistance when pierced with the tip of a sharp knife.

While the potatoes are boiling, pat the herring fillets dry with paper towels and sprinkle them on both sides, as evenly as possible, with the lemon juice and salt.

Using a pastry brush or paper towel, coat the bottom and sides of a shallow baking dish, large enough to hold the herring fillets in one layer, with 1 tablespoon of the butter. Arrange the fillets in the dish and scatter the chopped onions evenly over the top. Cover the dish tightly with aluminum foil and bake in the middle of the oven for about 20 minutes or until the herring fillets are firm. Do not overcook.

Drain the potatoes and slice them into ¼-inch thick rounds. Arrange the slices of potato, overlapping them, on a heated serving platter. Using a spatula, remove the herring fillets from the baking dish and arrange them attractively on top of the potatoes. Keep the potatoes and herring warm in the turned-off oven.

In a small saucepan, quickly melt the remaining 5 tablespoons of butter. When the butter begins to foam, beat the mustard into it with a small whisk until it is completely incorporated. Pour the mustard butter over the herring and potatoes and serve at once.

Salt Herring and Potato Casserole
4 to 6 Servings

- 2 to 3 salted herring (about 1½ pounds)
- 1 tablespoon unsalted butter
- ¼ cup fine bread crumbs
- 6 medium-sized boiling potatoes, peeled and thinly sliced
- 2 medium-sized onions, thinly sliced
- Freshly ground black pepper
- 3 eggs
- 2 cups milk

One-dish meals of fish and potatoes are a tradition in Newfoundland homes. The mustard sauce in the sauce section of this book makes a great accompaniment, or you could simply serve a small bowl of good-quality mustard alongside.

Beginning the night before you wish to serve the casserole, place the salted herring in a shallow bowl and cover them with cold water. Soak the herring for at least 18 hours, changing the water once or twice during the soaking period.

Preheat the oven to 350°F.

Clean, skin, fillet and trim the salted herrings. Cut the fillets into ½-inch pieces. Butter the inside of a 2-quart casserole dish. Add the bread crumbs and tilt the dish to coat. Fill the dish with alternating layers of potatoes, onions and herring, sprinkling each layer with a generous grinding of black pepper.

In a large bowl, beat the eggs together with the milk. Pour the mixture over the ingredients in the casserole dish. Bake the casserole for about 1 hour, or until the potatoes are cooked. Serve the casserole hot, directly from the dish.

LOBSTER

When I was very young, my grandfather caught lobsters and processed them in his small canning factory on Bonavista Bay. The parts of the lobster that didn't go into the cans ended up on the dinner table so often that one of my aunts refused to eat lobster ever again. The shells were used as fertilizer for the garden and I even remember my grandmother feeding lobster to her hens. I never tired of lobster though, and I still look forward with great anticipation to the opening of the lobster season each May.

Baited with fish or shellfish, lobsters are taken in wooden crate-like traps or "pots" sunk to the ocean floor with a weight and marked with a buoy. The pots are divided into two sections. In Newfoundland, these are called the "kitchen", the section where the bait is placed, and the "parlour", where it's next to impossible for the lobster to escape.

Described by many gourmets as the choicest lobster in the world, the *homarus americanus*, or American lobster, resides all around the coast of Newfoundland and Labrador and is a very important species in the inshore fishery. Lobsters live in deep water in winter, returning to shallower depths in spring. Commercially caught lobsters usually weigh between one and three pounds, although they have been known to grow to nearly fifty pounds.

Lobsters have greenish-black shells that turn red when cooked. They have two claws, the "crusher" being larger and heavier. The smaller claw is called the "ripper". Before sale, both claws of live lobsters are usually immobilized with wooden pegs or thick rubber bands. When selecting a live lobster, make sure it is lively and the tail curls tightly under the body. Lobsters may be kept alive for twelve hours or so if wrapped in moist newspaper and refrigerated. Frozen lobster tails and canned lobster meat are also available in many markets.

Lobster meat is lean and firm-textured. Except for the shell and the small stomach sac, which lies behind the head, all of the lobster is edible. The black roe, called "coral" (it turns red when cooked), and the green liver, called "tomalley", are both prized by most lobster fanciers.

Lobsters should not be overcooked or the meat will become tough. For boiled or steamed lobsters, about fifteen minutes per pound is sufficient.

STEAMED LOBSTER

4 SERVINGS

- 1 cup white wine
- 2 cups water
- 2 tablespoons freshly squeezed lemon juice
- 2 cloves garlic, coarsely chopped
- 1 bay leaf
- 1½ teaspoons sea salt
- 4 1½-pound lobsters

Choose a pot that is large enough to hold all the lobsters with ample room and is equipped with a tight-fitting lid (I use my preserving kettle).

Combine the wine, water, lemon juice, garlic, bay leaf and salt in the pot. Place a rack in the bottom of the pot (a cake rack will do nicely). Bring the mixture to a rolling boil over high heat. Put the lobsters in the pot, head first, and quickly cover with the lid. Begin timing as soon as the liquid comes to a boil again. Cook the lobsters for 20 minutes.

Remove the lobsters from the pot with large tongs. Set them aside until just cool enough to handle before removing the claw-restraining pegs or rubber bands.

Newfoundlanders usually speak of cooking lobsters as a "lobster boil", but rather than boiling them, I prefer this method of steaming. It's less messy for the home cook because the pot won't boil over and water won't become trapped inside the shell to squirt out when the lobster is cut or pulled apart. Another advantage is that the flavourful steaming liquid may be strained and saved to use in a soup or sauce.

A kitchen timer is useful here. Colour is not a good indication of when the lobsters are done because they often turn bright red within seconds of being placed in the pot. Twenty minutes is usually sufficient for one-and-one-half-pound lobsters, but if you're in doubt, use a heavy oven mitt to protect your hand from steam and pull off one of the little feeler claws. If it twists off easily, the lobsters are done. If your lobsters are larger, add five minutes for each extra one-quarter pound.

LOBSTER-STUFFED EGGS
12 HORS D'OEUVRES

- 6 hard-cooked large eggs
- 3 tablespoons mayonnaise
- ½ cup cooked lobster meat, finely chopped
- 1 teaspoon finely chopped onion
- ½ teaspoon dry mustard
- ½ teaspoon lemon juice
- Salt
- Freshly ground black pepper
- Paprika
- Small parsley sprigs for garnish

Cut a very small slice off both ends of the eggs (so they will stand up) and cut the eggs in half crosswise. With a small spoon, carefully remove the yolks from the eggs. Set the egg whites aside on a platter.

In a small food processor or blender, pulse together the egg yolks, mayonnaise, lobster, onion, mustard and lemon juice until smooth. Season the mixture to taste with salt and freshly ground pepper.

Transfer the lobster filling to a pastry bag fitted with a large decorative tip. Pipe the filling evenly into the egg whites, mounding it up in the centre. Sprinkle the stuffed eggs with a light dusting of paprika and garnish each with a small sprig of parsley.

This version of devilled eggs is an old Newfoundland recipe that I've modified only by the use of more modern kitchen equipment to achieve a smoother consistency. It's a great way to stretch a small amount of leftover steamed lobster, or canned lobster may be used. The recipe easily could be doubled for a buffet table.

Except for the garnish, the stuffed eggs may be made up to six hours ahead of time and refrigerated, covered with plastic wrap. To keep the wrap from marring the top of the egg stuffing, I stick thin toothpicks into the centre of the eggs. The parsley will cover the holes made by the toothpicks.

LOBSTER AND FIDDLEHEAD SALAD
4 TO 6 SERVINGS

- 10 ounces fresh fiddleheads, or frozen fiddleheads, thawed
- ¼ cup sour cream
- 1 tablespoon mayonnaise
- 1 teaspoon finely chopped fresh parsley
- 2 teaspoons finely chopped fresh tarragon leaves, or ½ teaspoon dried tarragon
- 2 teaspoons green pickle relish
- ¼ cup finely chopped red onion
- 2 hard-cooked eggs, coarsely chopped
- Salt
- Freshly ground black pepper
- 1 pound cooked fresh lobster meat, or canned frozen lobster meat, thawed
- Lettuce leaves
- Lemon wedges for garnish

What could be more east-coast Canadian than lobster and fiddleheads? Here they are combined in a fresh salad that makes a wonderful luncheon.

Fiddleheads are the edible fronds of ostrich ferns and get their name because they look like little violin heads. They appear early in the spring and many Newfoundlanders harvest them from the wild for use as a vegetable. They should always be washed in several changes of cold water because dirt may be trapped inside the tightly curled fronds.

In a medium-sized saucepan of boiling water, cook the fiddleheads just until they are tender-crisp. (Test by taking one out of the water and biting into it. Fresh fiddleheads will take a little longer than frozen, thawed.) Drain the fiddleheads in a colander and run them under cold water for a minute or 2 to set their green colour. Drain the fiddleheads well and dry them on paper towels.

In a large bowl, whisk together the sour cream and mayonnaise. Stir in the parsley, tarragon, green pickle relish, onion and chopped eggs to combine well. Add the lobster and fiddleheads and toss to combine with the dressing. Taste for seasoning and add salt and freshly ground black pepper. Cover the bowl and refrigerate for at least 1 hour to allow the flavours to blend.

To serve, line a platter with lettuce leaves. Heap the salad on the platter and garnish it with the lemon wedges.

GRILLED LOBSTER WITH TARRAGON BUTTER
4 SERVINGS

- ¾ cup unsalted butter
- ¼ cup freshly squeezed lemon juice
- 1 teaspoon finely grated lemon zest
- 2 tablespoons finely chopped fresh tarragon leaves
- Salt
- Freshly ground black pepper
- 4 live lobsters, each about 1½ pounds
- Lemon wedges for garnish

You can kill a lobster without cooking it by severing its spine at the joint where the body and tail sections meet. But, since so many people are squeamish about that procedure, I'm recommending a brief boil before grilling.

Prepare the barbecue for moderately high heat.

In a small heavy saucepan, over low heat, stir together the butter, lemon juice and lemon zest until the butter melts. Stir in the tarragon leaves. Season the mixture to taste with salt and pepper. Set the pan at edge of the grill to keep the sauce warm.

Bring a large pot (or 2 pots if one is not large enough) of well-salted water to a boil. Plunge in the lobsters head first and boil them for about 4 minutes. (This kills the lobsters, but they won't be cooked.) Using tongs, transfer the lobsters to a work surface.

Using a large heavy knife or cleaver, split the lobsters in half lengthwise. Remove the stomach sac from the head, but leave any coral (roe) or tomalley (liver) intact. Gash each claw once with the sharp knife or cleaver. Brush the cut side of the each lobster with 1 tablespoon of the tarragon-butter sauce.

Grill the lobsters, shell side down, for about 5 minutes, brushing once or twice with a little more of the tarragon-butter sauce. Turn the lobsters so that the cut side is down and continue to grill until the lobster meat is just opaque but still juicy, about 3 or 4 minutes longer.

Transfer the lobsters to 4 heated plates. Garnish with lemon wedges. Pour the remaining sauce into a heated sauceboat and serve.

LOBSTER BISQUE
4 TO 6 SERVINGS

This bisque is rich, so a small serving
is plenty for a soup course.

- 2 1-pound live lobsters, preferably females
- 3 tablespoons unsalted butter
- 1 medium-sized leek, white and pale green parts only, coarsely chopped
- 1 large celery stalk, sliced
- 1 medium-sized carrot, sliced
- 1 whole head garlic, cut in half crosswise
- 1 large sprig fresh tarragon, or 1 teaspoon dried tarragon
- 1 bay leaf

- 10 whole black peppercorns
- ½ cup cognac, or other good French brandy
- ½ cup dry sherry
- 4 cups basic fish stock (see recipe index)
- ¼ cup tomato paste

Cook the lobsters according to the recipe for steamed lobsters. Transfer them to a large bowl and reserve 2 cups of the cooking liquid. Cool the lobsters just until they can be easily handled. Working over the bowl to catch all the juices, twist off the tails and claws and crack them to remove the lobster meat. Coarsely chop the meat and refrigerate it, covered. Reserve the juices. Remove any coral (waxy red roe) from the lobster bodies. With a fork, mash the coral together with 1 tablespoon of the butter. Then push the mixture through a fine sieve into a small bowl and reserve it, covered and refrigerated.

Coarsely chop and crush the lobster shells and bodies. Heat the remaining 2 tablespoons butter in a large heavy pot over moderately high heat. Add the chopped lobster shells and bodies and sauté them for about 10 minutes. Add

the next 7 ingredients. Stir in the brandy and sherry. Bring the mixture to a boil and boil until most of the liquid has evaporated. Add the stock, the reserved 2 cups of cooking liquid and the reserved lobster juices. Reduce the heat to a slow simmer and simmer, partially covered, for 1 hour.

Strain the soup through a sieve set over a large saucepan, pressing down hard on the solids. Discard the solids. Whisk in the tomato paste. Bring the soup to a simmer and simmer until it is reduced to about 3½ cups. Stir in the cornstarch-and-water mixture and simmer until slightly thickened, about 2 minutes longer. Stir in the lobster meat, cream and reserved coral and cook gently, stirring, just to heat through. Taste and adjust the seasonings. Ladle the bisque into heated bowls and serve.

LOBSTER NEWBURG
6 SERVINGS

- 3 2-pound live lobsters
- ¼ cup unsalted butter
- 3 tablespoons medium-dry sherry
- 3 tablespoons cognac, or other good French brandy
- 1½ cups heavy cream
- Pinch freshly grated nutmeg
- ⅛ teaspoon cayenne
- ½ teaspoon salt
- 4 large egg yolks
- 6 large frozen vol-au-vent shells

This classic rich dish is traditionally served over toast points, but I prefer to serve it in vol-au-vent (puff-pastry shells), which may be purchased frozen in most large supermarkets.

Bring a large pot (or 2 pots if one is not large enough) of well-salted water to a boil. Plunge in the lobsters head first and boil them for about 4 minutes. (This kills the lobsters, but they won't be cooked.) Using tongs, transfer the lobsters to a work surface.

When the lobsters are just cool enough to handle, twist off the claws where they join the body and crack them with a lobster cracker or hammer. Remove the claw meat and cut it into ½-inch pieces. Reserve the meat on a plate. Remove the tail meat from the lobsters, cut it into ½-inch pieces and add it to the claw meat. Reserve the lobster bodies for shellfish stock or bisque. (Tightly wrapped, they may be frozen for a week or two.)

In a heavy non-reactive saucepan over moderate heat, melt the butter and sauté the lobster meat, stirring occasionally, for about 2 minutes. Add 2 tablespoons of the sherry and 2

tablespoons of the brandy and cook the mixture, stirring, for 2 minutes longer. Using a slotted spoon, transfer the cooked lobster meat to a dish and reserve it. Add the cream to the saucepan and boil the mixture until it is reduced to about 1 cup. Reduce the heat to low and stir in the remaining sherry, brandy, nutmeg, cayenne and salt.

In a bowl, beat the egg yolks until they are pale lemon-coloured. Stir ½ cup of the sauce into the egg yolks. Then pour the egg-yolk mixture back into the remaining sauce. Bring the sauce to a boil over moderate heat, whisking constantly, until it coats a spoon thickly. Taste and adjust the seasonings.

Meanwhile, bake the *vol-au-vent* according to the package directions. Just before serving, stir the reserved lobster meat into the sauce and cook gently to heat through. Divide the mixture equally among the pastry shells.

LOBSTER TAILS WITH SHERRY-GINGER SAUCE
4 SERVINGS

- 2 cups best-quality dry sherry
- 2 tablespoons liquid honey
- 3 tablespoons extra-virgin olive oil
- ½ teaspoon ground ginger, or to taste
- ½ cup unsalted butter, softened
- 1 large shallot, quartered
- 2 large cloves garlic, halved
- ½ teaspoon salt
- ½ teaspoon freshly ground black pepper
- 4 10-ounce uncooked lobster tails, thawed if frozen, cut in half lengthwise

For those times when you want to splurge, this is a sensational dish. The flavoured butter keeps the grilled lobster meat very moist and the sherry-ginger sauce is so delicious you could almost drink it on its own.

In a non-reactive saucepan, bring the sherry to a boil over high heat. Reduce the heat to moderate and simmer the sherry until it is reduced to ½ cup, about 6 or 7 minutes. Add the honey and stir until it is dissolved. Remove the mixture from the heat and, 1 tablespoon at a time, beat in the olive oil, blending to emulsify (an immersion mixer is useful for this). Add the ginger and taste for seasoning. Set the sauce aside.

In a food processor, combine the butter, shallot, garlic, salt and pepper. Blend until smooth. Spread about 1 teaspoon of the mixture evenly over the cut side of each lobster tail half. Transfer the remaining seasoned butter to small saucepan.

Prepare a barbecue grill for moderately high heat. Set the saucepan with the butter at edge of the grill until the butter is melted and warmed through.

Grill the lobster tails, shell side down, for about 5 minutes, brushing occasionally with the melted butter. Turn the lobster so that the cut side is down and continue to grill until the lobster meat is just opaque but still juicy, about 3 minutes longer.

Meanwhile gently reheat the sherry-ginger sauce, whisking it to recombine the ingredients.

Arrange 2 lobster tail halves, shell side down, on each of 4 heated plates. Pour the sauce over and around the lobster and serve immediately.

MACKEREL

I grew up convinced that I didn't like mackerel. Then my friend Dave spent a summer among people who caught and cooked this fish and came back not only with some fresh mackerel, but also with some wonderful recipes that changed my mind.

The mackerel, *scomber scombrus*, is a highly migratory fish found on both sides of the Atlantic and in waters all around Newfoundland. Commercially caught mackerel are from fourteen to eighteen inches in length and weigh from about one to two and one-half pounds, although they have been known to grow up to nearly eight pounds.

Atlantic mackerel are open-ocean fish with voracious feeding habits, eating small finfish, squid, crustaceans and a large variety of plankton-like organisms. They travel in schools that often contain thousands of fish of approximately the same size.

The mackerel's streamlined body allows it to swim at high speeds for extended periods of time. The upper half of the body is iridescent blue-green with a dark, wavy band. The lower half and belly are silvery white. The mackerel's scales are small and smooth, giving a velvety texture to the skin.

Atlantic mackerel is delicious, but many people ignore it, as I once did, because of its fat content. This is a shame because the oil it contains is the heart-healthy omega-3 fatty acid.

The oiliness of mackerel can easily be overcome with the introduction of acid when the fish is cooked. Marinating the mackerel in citrus juice, cooking it with tomato or using a tart or spicy sauce are all good ways to lighten the flavour that the oil imparts to the fish.

Mackerel can be baked or broiled with great success. But the barbecue grill is a good way to bring out the best in the mackerel's flavor.

Because of its high oil content, fresh mackerel deteriorates rapidly and should be cooked as soon as possible after catching or purchasing. However, it freezes well.

Broiled Mackerel with Basil

4 Servings

- 1 cup finely chopped fresh basil leaves
- ½ cup finely chopped fresh parsley
- 2 large garlic cloves, minced
- 4 tablespoons extra-virgin olive oil
- 3 tablespoons water
- 2 tablespoons freshly squeezed lemon juice
- Salt
- Freshly ground black pepper
- 4 8-ounce mackerel fillets with skin
- Lemon wedges

Broiled tomato halves drizzled with a little olive oil make a wonderful accompaniment to the fish. They can go under the broiler at the same time as the mackerel, but watch them carefully so they don't scorch.

Preheat the broiler.

In a small bowl, stir together the basil, parsley and garlic. Add 3 tablespoons of the oil and stir it in well. Blend in the water, lemon juice, and salt and pepper to taste.

Arrange the mackerel fillets, skin sides down, in an oiled shallow baking pan. Brush the fish with the remaining tablespoon of oil and season with salt and pepper.

Broil the fish 5 to 6 inches from the heat, without turning, until just cooked through, about 7 minutes.

Place a fillet of fish on each of 4 heated serving plates. Quickly spread some of the basil sauce over the fish and garnish with lemon wedges.

MACKEREL CASSEROLE
4 SERVINGS

I love the crisp crunchy topping and bright electric flavours of this easy-to-make casserole.

- 3 medium-sized vine-ripened tomatoes, peeled, seeded and sliced ¼-inch thick
- 2 medium-sized onions, thinly sliced and separated into rings
- 4 cloves garlic, finely chopped
- ½ teaspoon fennel seeds, crushed
- ½ teaspoon dried summer savory
- 2 bay leaves, preferably fresh
- Salt
- Freshly ground black pepper
- 6 tablespoons extra-virgin olive oil
- 1½ pounds small mackerel, cleaned with heads and tails removed
- ½ cup dry white wine
- ¾ cup coarse bread crumbs, made from day-old homemade-type white bread

Preheat the oven to 375°F.

Choose a baking and serving dish about 3 or 4 inches deep and just large enough to hold the mackerel in one layer. Layer half the tomato slices on the bottom of the dish. Press half the onion rings on top of the tomatoes. Scatter the tomatoes and onions with half the garlic, half the fennel seeds and half the savory. Press the bay leaves into the top and season lightly with salt and pepper. Drizzle about 2 tablespoons of the olive oil over all and press all the mackerel into place over the vegetables and herbs. Drizzle another 2 tablespoons of olive oil over the mackerel and season them lightly with salt and pepper. Scatter the remaining garlic over the mackerel. Cover with the remaining onion slices and the remaining fennel and savory. Press the remaining tomato slices evenly over the top. Season the tomatoes with a little more salt and pepper. Scatter the bread crumbs evenly over all and drizzle with the remaining olive oil.

Place the dish in the oven and bake, uncovered, for about 45 minutes, or until the crumb topping is crisp and golden.

Serve directly from the baking dish.

MACKEREL WITH FENNEL MAYONNAISE

4 SERVINGS

- 1 tablespoon fennel seeds
- ¼ cup mayonnaise, preferably homemade (see recipe index)
- 2 tablespoons freshly squeezed lemon juice
- 2 large cloves garlic, minced
- Salt
- Coarsely ground or cracked black pepper
- 4 6- to 8-ounce skinless mackerel fillets

This flavourful dish is highly seasoned and best served with a simple accompaniment such as boiled potatoes or steamed rice.

Preheat the broiler and arrange a rack about 4 inches from the heat. Oil a shallow baking pan large enough to hold the mackerel fillets in one layer.

In a heavy small dry frying pan over moderate heat, toast the fennel seeds, stirring, until they are fragrant, about 2 minutes. Using a spice grinder or mortar and pestle, pulverize the fennel seeds to a coarse powder.

In a small bowl, stir the pulverized fennel seeds into the mayonnaise along with the lemon juice and minced garlic. Combine the mixture well and stir in salt and coarsely ground or cracked pepper to taste.

Arrange the mackerel fillets in the prepared pan and spread the fennel mayonnaise evenly over the top of each fillet. Broil the fillets on 1 side only, until just cooked through, about 8 minutes.

MUSSELS

I think the best mussels I ever ate were wild ones my mother and I plucked from the seaweed one summer day near her home in Bonavista Bay. Boiled in a big old pot of bay water on the beach and eaten with Mom's homemade bread, they were sweet and juicy and tasted of the sea.

It's not unusual to see wild mussels growing on seaweed, rocks and piers all around Newfoundland coastal areas, but most commercial mussels are now cultivated. Although farmed mussels lack some of the wild mussel mystique, they are generally sand-free and of uniform size and taste.

The blue mussel, *mytilus edulis*, is the species cultivated in Newfoundland waters. They are bivalve molluscs that grow quickly and profusely, two traits that make them ideal for aquaculture. They are typically cultured on 600-foot ropes, anchored securely at both ends and supported by floats tied at intervals along their length.

Clamped tight in its secret world, the mussel literally clings to life by threads, called byssal threads, which anchor it firmly to its home. Wound together, these threads form what we call the mussel's "beard".

Mussels are suspension feeders, that is, they feed by actively filtering tiny particles from the water. Their oval shells, blue-black on the outside and pearly on the inside, are joined by a rubbery hinged ligament.

When buying fresh cultivated mussels or gathering your own from the wild, take only those that are tightly closed or that close up tightly when gently tapped. Mussels will keep for several days, loosely wrapped and refrigerated. When using wild mussels, I like to soak them for an hour or two in cold water to which a small handful of coarse salt and an equivalent amount of easy-blend flour has been added. The theory is that while the mussels ingest the flour, making them fatter and more succulent, they also disgorge any sand.

Before cooking, mussels should be scrubbed and their beards removed, but wait until the last minute to do this or the mussels will die. The mussels may be shelled raw or steamed or grilled just until the shells open.

Mussel meat ranges in colour from pale to deep orange with an edible black fringe. It is soft and mild in flavour. Mussels may be added to casseroles, soups, stews or salads or used as a garnish for other seafood.

MARINATED MUSSELS
ABOUT 1 QUART

- 5 pounds mussels in their shells, scrubbed and debearded
- 1½ cups water
- 1 large onion, very thinly sliced (about 1 cup)
- 4 cloves garlic, peeled and crushed with the side of a heavy knife
- ½ cup cider vinegar, or white-wine vinegar
- 2 teaspoons mixed pickling spices
- 1 teaspoon salt

In the summer, when wild mussels were plentiful, Newfoundlanders traditionally bottled them in a brine solution to preserve them for winter. Now that farmed mussels are available in markets almost all year, this practice is no longer so prevalent.

Because the mussels in this recipe aren't processed and sealed, they won't keep as long as the traditional preserved mussels, but they will keep for a week or more. They may be served on lettuce leaves as a first course or speared on cocktail picks as an accompaniment to drinks.

Combine the mussels and water in a large heavy non-reactive pot. Over high heat, bring the water to a boil. Cover the pot tightly and steam the mussels over the high heat for 5 or 6 minutes, or until they are all opened. With a slotted spoon, transfer the mussels, in their shells, to a large bowl. Discard any mussels that do not open. Reserve the liquid remaining in the pot.

Strain the liquid in the pot and any liquid that has accumulated around the mussels in the bowl through a sieve lined with a double thickness of dampened cheesecloth. Measure 1½ cups of the liquid into a medium-sized non-reactive saucepan and set the saucepan aside.

When the mussels are cool enough to handle, remove and discard their shells. Place about ¼ of the mussels in a 1-quart wide-mouth jar. Spread about ¼ of the onion slices over them and set a clove of crushed garlic on top. Repeat this procedure three more times, alternating layers of mussels with onions and garlic until you have arranged all the mussels in the jar.

Add the vinegar, pickling spices and salt to the reserved liquid. Bring it to a boil over high heat and cook briskly, uncovered, for 2 minutes. Slowly pour the hot mixture over the mussels. Cool the mussels to room temperature, then cover the jar tightly and refrigerate for at least 3 days before serving.

CURRIED MUSSELS ON THE HALF SHELL
ABOUT 4 DOZEN SMALL HORS D'OEUVRES

These tasty little tidbits are marvelous party fare, especially since most of the preparation can be done ahead of time.

- 1½ teaspoons curry paste, preferably Thai-style
- 2 tablespoons unseasoned rice vinegar
- 1 tablespoon freshly squeezed lime juice
- 1 tablespoon Asian sesame oil
- 4 tablespoons olive oil
- 2 pounds mussels, preferably cultivated
- ¼ cup minced shallots or red onion
- 1 medium-sized carrot, cut into ¼-inch dice
- 1 celery stalk, cut into ¼-inch dice
- 1 small red bell pepper, cut into ¼-inch dice
- Salt
- ¼ cup chopped fresh cilantro (also called coriander)

In a large bowl, stir together the curry paste, vinegar, lime juice, sesame oil and 3 tablespoons of the olive oil.

In a large heavy frying pan, heat the remaining tablespoon of olive oil over moderately high heat until it is hot but not smoking. Add the shallots, carrot, celery and pepper and sauté the vegetables, stirring, until they are soft but not brown. Add salt to taste. Add the vegetables to the curry mixture, stirring to combine.

Scrub the mussels and remove their beards. In a large heavy pot, steam the mussels in ½ cup of water, covered, over moderately high heat, for 5 to 7 minutes, or until they are all opened. Drain them in a colander. Discard any unopened mussels.

When the mussels are cool enough to handle, remove them from their shells. Reserve half of each shell. Add the mussels to the curry-vegetable mixture, stirring gently to coat. Marinate the mussels, covered and refrigerated, for at least 4 hours and up to 1 day. Wash the reserved the shell halves and set them aside.

Just before serving, stir the chopped cilantro into the mussel mixture. Using a teaspoon, fill each reserved shell with a mussel and some curried vegetables. To serve, arrange the filled mussel shells close together on a large platter.

ROASTED MUSSELS
4 FIRST-COURSE SERVINGS

- 1½ pounds very fresh mussels in their shells, scrubbed and debearded
- Freshly ground black pepper (optional)

After collecting wild mussels, many people like to steam them in seawater over a fire on the beach, but some Newfoundlanders prefer to roast the mussels in an iron frying pan. Even if you're nowhere near a beach, you can still enjoy these mussels, cooked only in the moisture of their own briny elixir of the sea.

There are no complicated preparations or ingredients here, just mussels, pure and simple. These should be eaten as soon as they have opened, while they are still moist. They may be transferred to plates and served at the table, but I suggest they be eaten informally, with friends standing around the stove.

If the mussels are wild ones, discard any with broken shells or shells that feel too heavy (there may be nothing but sand enclosed between the shells).

Using no oil or fat, heat a very large heavy frying pan, preferably of cast iron, over high heat. The pan will be hot enough when a drop of water sizzles and evaporates immediately. Spoon all the mussels into the frying pan and begin shaking the pan back and forth over the heat. The mussels should begin to open almost immediately. Continue shaking the pan until all the mussels have opened.

As soon as all the mussels have opened, remove the pan from the heat. If desired, sprinkle the mussels with a grinding of black pepper. Serve immediately.

Mussels in Herb Sauce
6 First-Course Servings

*Here's an uncomplicated and delicious
starter that's best made with the
freshest herbs available.*

- 3 tablespoons extra-virgin olive oil
- ½ cup finely chopped shallots
- 2 cloves garlic, minced
- 1 tablespoon finely chopped fresh thyme leaves
- 1 tablespoon finely chopped fresh tarragon leaves
- 1 tablespoon finely chopped fresh basil leaves
- 2 small bay leaves, preferably fresh
- 1½ cups dry white wine
- 1 cup basic fish stock (see recipe index), or substitute bottled clam juice
- ¼ cup heavy cream
- 2½ pounds mussels in their shells, scrubbed and debearded

In a heavy saucepan over moderate heat, sauté the shallots, stirring until they are soft but not brown, about 5 minutes. Add the garlic, thyme, tarragon, basil, bay leaves, 1 cup of the wine, clam juice and cream. Bring the mixture to a boil, reduce the heat and simmer, uncovered, until the mixture is reduced to 1 cup, about 10 minutes.

Meanwhile, bring the remaining ½ cup of wine to a boil in a large non-reactive pot. Add the mussels. Cover the pot tightly and steam the mussels over high heat for about 5 minutes, or just until they are opened. With a slot-ted spoon, transfer the mussels, in their shells, to 6 heated bowls. Discard any mussels that do not open.

Using a large sieve lined with a double thickness of dampened cheesecloth, strain all the wine and mussel juices from the large pot into the simmering herb sauce. Bring the sauce to a boil over high heat and continue to boil, stirring, until it is slightly reduced and thickened, about 3 minutes. Taste and adjust the seasonings before pouring in equal amounts over the mussels.

MUSSELS IN LEMON CREAM SAUCE
4 FIRST-COURSE SERVINGS

The sauce here is vibrant, lemony and full-flavoured, making for a rich first course best served before a light meal.

- 4 tablespoons unsalted butter, softened
- 6 large cloves garlic, minced
- 1 large shallot, minced
- ¼ cup finely chopped fresh parsley leaves
- 2 tablespoons freshly squeezed lemon juice
- Salt
- Freshly ground black pepper
- 4 medium-sized vine-ripened tomatoes
- 1 teaspoon finely grated lemon zest
- 3 pounds cultivated mussels, scrubbed and debearded
- 1 cup dry white wine
- 1½ cups heavy cream

In a medium-sized bowl, stir together the butter, half the garlic, the shallot, half the parsley, the lemon juice, and salt and pepper to taste. Core the tomatoes, remove the seeds and cut them into ¼-inch dice.

In a 6-quart heavy saucepan melt the seasoned butter over moderate heat. Add the lemon zest and the remaining garlic and cook, stirring, 30 seconds. Add the mussels and cook, stirring, 1 minute. Add the wine, cream, and salt and pepper to taste and simmer, covered, until the mussels are opened, about 5 minutes. Discard any unopened mussels.

Stir in the tomato and remaining parsley. Divide the mixture among 4 heated soup plates and serve immediately.

Mussels in Tomato-Wine Sauce
4 Servings

- ¼ cup olive oil
- ¾ cup finely chopped onions
- 1 tablespoon finely chopped garlic
- ¼ cup finely chopped celery
- 1 28-ounce can of tomatoes, preferably Italian plum tomatoes, coarsely chopped, juice reserved
- 1 tablespoon finely chopped fresh basil leaves, or 1 teaspoon dried basil
- ½ teaspoon salt
- Freshly ground black pepper
- 2 cups dry white wine
- 5 pounds mussels in their shells, scrubbed and debearded
- 1 teaspoon grated lemon zest
- 2 tablespoons finely chopped fresh parsley leaves

I make this dish often because it contains my favourite complementary ingredients: tomatoes, garlic, olive oil and white wine. Provide spoons and a loaf of good country-style bread to get every last drop of the flavourful juices.

In a heavy saucepan, heat the oil over moderate heat. Add the onions and garlic and cook, stirring, for about 5 minutes, or until they are soft but not brown. Add the celery, the tomatoes and their juice, the basil, salt and a generous grinding of black pepper. Bring the mixture to a boil, partially cover the pot, reduce the heat to low and simmer for 10 minutes.

Meanwhile, bring the wine to a boil in a large non-reactive pot. Add the mussels. Cover the pot tightly and steam the mussels over high heat for about 5 minutes, or just until they are opened. With a slotted spoon, transfer the mussels, in their shells, to 4 large heated soup plates or pasta bowls. Discard any mussels that do not open.

Using a large sieve lined with a double thickness of dampened cheesecloth, strain all the wine and mussel juices from the large pot into the simmering tomato sauce. Bring the sauce to a boil over high heat and continue to boil, stirring, until it is slightly reduced and thickened, about 3 minutes. Taste and adjust the seasonings.

Pour the sauce, in equal amounts, over the mussels. Sprinkle each serving with ¼ teaspoon grated lemon zest and some of the parsley. Serve immediately.

MUSSELS WITH ALMONDS AND GARLIC

4 SERVINGS

- ½ cup slivered almonds
- 5 tablespoons unsalted butter
- 6 large cloves garlic, finely minced
- 4 pounds mussels, preferably cultivated
- ½ cup finely chopped fresh flat-leafed parsley leaves
- 1½ cups dry white wine
- Salt
- Freshly ground black pepper

An interesting play of flavours and textures makes this an unusual but truly delicious dish.

Preheat the oven to 425°F.

Place the almonds on a small baking sheet and toast them in the middle of the oven until they just begin to turn golden, about 4 minutes. Set the almonds aside.

In a small frying pan, melt 2 tablespoons of the butter over moderate heat. Stir in the minced garlic and cook it, stirring, for about 5 minutes or until it is soft but not brown.

Scrub the mussels well and remove their beards.

In an ovenproof pan large enough to hold all the mussels, combine the mussels, garlic, parsley, wine and remaining butter. Season the mixture with salt and pepper. Roast the mussels for 15 minutes, uncovered, stirring once halfway through the roasting or until the mussels have opened. Discard any unopened mussels. Add the almonds and toss to combine. Taste for seasoning and serve the mussels in heated bowls.

OCEAN PERCH

The first time I saw a whole, fresh ocean perch at a fish market, I was almost convinced it was staring at me. That's because the fish's beautifully bright reddish-orange colouring makes its large black eyes stand out in such contrast.

The fish marketed as "ocean perch", *sebastes mainus* or *sebastes mentella*, also known as redfish, rosefish or sea perch, is not a perch at all, but a member of the rockfish family. It should not be confused with freshwater perch or with redfish from the Gulf of Mexico, which are drums.

A deepwater groundfish that travels in large schools, ocean perch can be found in both inshore and offshore waters all around Newfoundland and Labrador, inhabiting a rock bottom that is densely covered with seaweed. Caught mainly by trawling, ocean perch typically weigh from one to two pounds, but can grow larger.

Ocean perch is a slow-growing species and differs from most other fish in that it bears its young live.

Ocean perch has a slightly sweet and mild taste. The texture is moderately firm, lean, moist and flaky. The flesh is white, though not as snowy white as cod, with a reddish tinge on the surface.

Skinned ocean perch with the fat line removed has the most delicate flavour and will keep better. Large ocean perch, those over three pounds, develop a coarser texture. Whole fish may have bulging eyes and distended air bladders, a result of being brought up from the depths of the ocean floor. This is not an indication of poor quality.

Ocean perch is marvellously versatile. It may be poached, grilled, fried or steamed and is adaptable to almost any recipe for white firm-fleshed fish. Its mild flavour is complemented by almost any kind of sauce from a simple herbed butter to a highly seasoned and more complex accompaniment. It is also delicious served cold with mayonnaise.

Nut-Crusted Ocean Perch
4 to 6 Servings

*A coating of pecans seals in the flavour
and gives the fish a wonderful crunch.*

- 2 eggs
- 1 tablespoon milk
- 1½ pounds ocean perch fillets
- ½ teaspoon salt
- Freshly ground black pepper
- ½ cup all-purpose flour
- 1 cup finely chopped unsalted pecans
- 3 tablespoons unsalted butter
- 2 tablespoons vegetable oil
- Lemon wedges

In a shallow bowl, beat the eggs and milk together lightly with a fork. Pat the fillets dry and sprinkle them evenly with the salt and a few grindings of black pepper. Spread the flour on one piece of waxed paper and the chopped pecans on another. One at a time, dip the fillets in the flour, shaking gently to remove the excess. Immerse the fillets in the egg mixture, turning them to coat. Then place them on the nuts, turning them until they are evenly coated on both sides. Arrange the fillets in one layer on a wire rack set over a baking sheet. Refrigerate the coated fillets for at least 30 minutes to firm up the coating.

In a large heavy frying pan, melt the butter and oil together over moderate heat. When the foam begins to subside, add 2 or 3 fillets to the pan, depending on their size. Do not crowd them. Fry the fillets for about 3 or 4 minutes on each side, turning them with a wide spatula. When they are done they should be golden brown, crisp and firm to the touch. Transfer the cooked fillets to a heated platter and keep them warm in a low oven while you fry the remaining fillets.

Serve the fillets garnished with lemon wedges.

OCEAN PERCH WITH TOMATOES AND LEEKS

4 SERVINGS

- ¼ cup olive oil
- 2 medium-sized leeks, white and pale green parts only, thinly sliced
- 2 large garlic cloves, minced
- 1 tablespoon chopped fresh thyme leaves, or 1 teaspoon dried thyme
- 1 bay leaf
- 1 cup basic fish stock (see recipe index)
- 1 tablespoon freshly squeezed lemon juice
- ½ cup dry white wine
- 1 14-ounce can of tomatoes, with juice, chopped
- Salt
- Freshly ground black pepper
- 8 ocean perch fillets (about 1½ pounds total)
- ½ cup all-purpose flour
- 1 tablespoon finely chopped parsley

This is best made with homemade fish stock, but if you don't have it, you may substitute powdered seafood stock made according to package directions or canned or bottled clam juice diluted with water to make it less salty.

In a large frying pan, heat 2 tablespoons of the oil over moderate heat. Add the leeks, garlic, thyme and bay leaf. Sauté the mixture for about 5 minutes until the leeks are tender. Add the fish stock, lemon juice and wine. Bring the mixture to a boil and boil for 5 minutes. Add the chopped tomatoes with their juice. Boil, about 10 minutes, stirring frequently, until the sauce is very thick. Season the sauce to taste with salt and pepper.

Meanwhile, place the flour in a shallow bowl or on a piece of waxed paper. Season it with salt and pepper. Dredge each fish fillet in the seasoned flour and shake off the excess.

In another large heavy frying pan, heat the remaining 2 tablespoons of oil over moderately high heat. Add the fish and sauté it about 2 minutes per side until it is golden brown and opaque in the centre. Transfer the fish to heated plates and spoon equal amounts of the sauce over each serving. Sprinkle a little parsley over each serving.

OCEAN PERCH WITH ORANGE SAUCE
4 SERVINGS

Citrus fruit juice and fennel seeds are combined with wine for an intense reduction of flavours.

- ½ cup freshly squeezed orange juice
- 2 tablespoons freshly squeezed lemon juice
- ½ cup dry white wine
- ½ cup finely chopped red onion
- 1 teaspoon fennel seeds
- 2 teaspoons grated orange zest
- 1 cup water
- 8 ocean perch fillets (about 1½ pounds)
- Salt
- Freshly ground black pepper
- 1 navel orange, peeled and sectioned

In a large non-reactive frying pan equipped with a cover, bring the orange juice, lemon juice, white wine, red onion, fennel seeds and orange zest to a boil over high heat. Continue to boil the mixture, stirring occasionally, until most of the liquid has evaporated, about 10 minutes.

Add the water and the fish fillets and bring to a simmer. Cover the pan, lower the heat and poach the fish fillets for about 7 minutes, or until they are cooked through.

With a wide slotted spoon or spatula, transfer the cooked ocean perch fillets to 4 heated plates and keep them warm in a low oven. Boil the poaching liquid rapidly until it is reduced to about ½ cup. Season the sauce with salt and pepper to taste.

To serve, pour the sauce through a fine sieve into a pitcher or measuring cup, pressing down hard on the ingredients. Discard the solids in the sieve. Quickly divide the sieved sauce equally over the servings of fish. Garnish the fish with sections of orange.

OYSTERS

Those of us who love oysters usually aren't just devotees; we're insatiable addicts. No mere six oysters on the half-shell will do. We want dozens at a time, preferably "*au naturel*": no sauce, just the oyster cupped in the lower half of its shell in its own briny-sweet liquor. That's the tradition in my husband's family before Christmas dinner, when my father-in-law shucks them over the sink and hands them around in turns.

The oyster native to the Atlantic coast is *crassostrea virginica*, commonly known as the Atlantic oyster or American oyster, although it goes by a number of other regional names.

Except in the earliest stages of development, oysters lack the power of locomotion. They lie motionless, attached to rocks or other hard objects, sometimes in great clusters. The two shells of the oyster differ in shape and together make a form a very tight seal. The cupped lower part accommodates the body, while the flat upper part acts like a lid. As long as the oyster keeps its shell closed, it can protect itself from predators and survive long periods of exposure to unfavorable water conditions and to air at low tide.

Oysters are an exotic shellfish species in Newfoundland. The water temperatures do not get high enough for them to spawn here and all spat (very young oysters) are imported, mainly from New Brunswick or Prince Edward Island. Oysters are now being farmed in several areas in Notre Dame Bay and on the south coast of the island. Since the best oysters are those that grow slowly and without overcrowding, it is hoped that the colder temperatures, which inhibit quick growth, and knowledgeable farming practices, will produce superior oysters.

Oysters purchased live in the shell should be tightly closed. If the shell gapes open and remains open when handled, the oyster is dead and unfit to eat. When buying shucked raw oysters, look for those in the clearest juice. They should be practically odour-free. Oysters in the shell, as well as those shucked and properly packed, should keep for a day or two in the refrigerator. Oysters are also available canned in brine and smoked and canned in oil.

Oysters may be eaten raw, baked, fried, grilled or used in stews and chowders. They should be cooked at a low temperature only until they plump up and the edges begin to curl. Overcooking makes oysters tough.

ANGELS ON HORSEBACK
2 DOZEN HORS D'OEUVRES

I don't know where this recipe comes from or who invented it, but I love both the name and these very tasty little appetizers.

- 12 thin bacon slices, cut in half crosswise
- 2 dozen fresh oysters, shucked
- Salt
- Freshly ground black pepper
- Paprika
- Fresh parsley sprigs for garnish
- Lemon wedges

Preheat the oven to 450°F.

In a large heavy frying pan, cook the bacon pieces over moderate heat, turning them frequently, until they are translucent but have not begun to brown. Set the bacon aside on paper towels to drain.

Sprinkle the oysters lightly with salt, pepper and paprika. Wrap a piece of bacon around each oyster and secure it with a wooden cocktail pick. Place the wrapped oysters on a rack in a shallow pan and bake, turning once, for about 10 minutes, or until the bacon is crisp on all sides.

Remove the picks and serve the angels on horseback on a platter garnished with the parsley sprigs and accompanied by lemon wedges.

SMOKED OYSTER BEIGNETS
ABOUT 4 DOZEN HORS D'OEUVRES

These make a great accompaniment to cocktails and they always disappear quickly.

- 2 3½-ounce cans smoked oysters, drained and chopped
- 1 cup milk
- ¾ teaspoon salt
- ¼ cup unsalted butter
- 1 cup all-purpose flour
- 3 eggs
- Vegetable oil for deep frying
- Cocktail sauce (see recipe index)

In a large heavy saucepan, combine the milk, salt and butter. Bring the mixture to a boil over high heat. Reduce the heat to moderate and add the flour all at once, stirring vigorously with a wooden spoon until the mixture forms a smooth ball and leaves the sides of the pan. Allow the mixture to cool for 5 minutes.

Add the eggs to the flour-and-milk mixture, one at a time, beating well after each addition. Stir in the oysters.

Pour the vegetable oil into a deep heavy saucepan or deep fryer to a depth of about 3 inches. Heat the oil to 375°F on a deep-frying thermometer. Working in small batches, drop teaspoons of the batter into the hot fat and fry them until they are golden brown. Using a slotted spoon, transfer the beignets to paper towels to drain and keep them warm in a low oven. Repeat the procedure with the remaining batter, making sure the oil returns to 375°F between each batch.

Serve the beignets hot, speared with toothpicks and accompanied by cocktail sauce for dipping.

OYSTER STEW
8 FIRST-COURSE SERVINGS

This is a simple first course that brings out the best of sweet and succulent oysters. The servings here are small because the stew is very rich.

- 1 quart shucked oysters, drained, with liquor reserved
- 4 cups light cream
- ½ teaspoon salt
- ½ teaspoon celery salt
- Pinch white pepper
- 8 teaspoons unsalted butter
- Small parsley sprigs for garnish

In a heavy 3- to 4-quart saucepan, combine the reserved oyster liquor with the cream. Heat the mixture gently, stirring, just until small bubbles appear around the edge of the pan. Reduce the heat to low and stir in the salt, celery salt and pepper. Add the oysters. Simmer the oysters gently, stirring occasionally, until the oysters plump up and their edges begin to curl. Taste and adjust seasonings.

To serve, place a teaspoon of butter in each of 8 individual heated soup bowls. Ladle in the oyster stew, garnish each serving with a small sprig of parsley and serve immediately.

OYSTERS BAKED WITH BRANDY BUTTER
4 FIRST-COURSE SERVINGS

Here meltingly tender oysters are served in a rich buttery sauce.

- 3 slices lean bacon, finely chopped
- 2 tablespoons minced shallot
- 3 tablespoons cognac, or other good-quality French brandy
- ¼ cup unsalted butter, softened
- 3 teaspoons minced parsley leaves, preferably flat-leaf parsley
- 1 dozen fresh oysters in their shells
- Coarse salt
- Lemon wedges

In a heavy frying pan, cook the bacon over moderate heat, stirring occasionally, until it has rendered all its fat and is beginning to crisp. Add the shallot and cook the mixture, stirring occasionally, until the shallot is softened. Stir in the brandy and cool the mixture to room temperature. In a small bowl stir together the bacon mixture, butter and parsley. The brandy butter may be prepared a day ahead, formed into a 6-inch-long log and chilled, wrapped tightly in plastic wrap.

Preheat the oven to 425°F.

Shuck the oysters, loosening each from the shell over a bowl to catch the liquor. Reserve the oyster liquor and the deeper half of each shell.

In a roasting pan large enough to hold all the oysters, spread coarse salt ¼ inch deep and nestle the deep shell halves into the salt to keep them level. Place an oyster in each shell. Sprinkle each oyster with about ½ teaspoon of the reserved oyster liquor. Cut the butter log into 12 equal pieces and place a piece on top of each oyster. If necessary, the oysters may be prepared up to this point several hours ahead and chilled, covered with plastic wrap.

Bake the oysters, about 10 minutes until they plump up and the butter is sizzling. Do not overbake.

While the oysters are baking, spread coarse salt ¼ inch deep on each of 4 plates. When the oysters are ready, carefully remove them from the pan and nestle 3 oysters in their shells into the salt on each plate. Garnish each plate with lemon wedges and serve immediately.

OYSTERS ROCKEFELLER
4 FIRST-COURSE SERVINGS

It is said that this dish is called Rockefeller because it is so rich.

- Coarse sea salt, or rock salt
- 2 dozen large oysters, shucked, with all their liquor and the deeper halves of the shells reserved
- 2 cups coarsely chopped green onions, with an inch or so of their green tops
- 2 cups coarsely chopped fresh parsley, preferably flat-leafed parsley
- 2 pounds fresh spinach leaves, washed, trimmed and patted dry
- ½ pound cold unsalted butter, cut into ½-inch bits
- 5 garlic cloves, minced
- ¾ cup all-purpose flour
- 3 tablespoons anchovy paste
- ½ teaspoon cayenne pepper
- 1½ teaspoons salt
- ¾ cup Pernod (anise-flavoured liqueur)

Preheat the oven to 400°F. Spread the coarse salt to a depth of about ½ inch in a very large shallow roasting pan. Place the pan in the oven to heat the salt while you prepare the oysters.

Over a large bowl, drain the oysters and their liquor through a fine sieve lined with a double thickness of dampened cheesecloth. Measure and reserve 3 cups of the oyster liquor. If there is less than 3 cups, add water to make up the amount. Transfer the oysters to a bowl and set them aside.

Scrub the deeper halves of the oyster shells, pat them dry and set them aside. In a food processor, pulse together the green onions, parsley and spinach. You will probably have to do this in batches.

In a large heavy non-reactive saucepan, melt the butter over moderate heat. Add the garlic and cook it for a minute or so, stirring. Do not let it brown. Add the flour and cook, stirring, for about 2 minutes. Stirring with a wire whisk, pour in the oyster liquor in a slow stream. Cook the mixture, whisking constantly, until it is thick and smooth. Stir in the anchovy paste, cayenne, salt and the onion-parsley-spinach mixture and Pernod. Simmer the sauce, for about 5 minutes uncovered, or until it is thick enough to hold its shape in a spoon. Taste and adjust the seasonings.

Nestle the reserved oyster shells into the heated salt and place an oyster in each shell. Spoon the sauce over the oysters, dividing it equally. Bake the oysters for about 15 minutes, or until they begin to curl at the edges and the sauce is delicately browned.

To serve, carefully place 6 of the oysters on each of 4 plates.

SCALLOPS

The beautiful fan-shaped scallop shell has been revered down through the ages. Buildings in ancient Pompeii were ornamented with scallop-shell designs. Poets have written about the scallop's beauty. Its symmetry and grace have inspired countless artists. During the crusades, pilgrims followed the route of St. James to Spain, where they gathered scallop shells to use as spoons and cups and tied them around their necks. Scallops are still often referred to as *coquilles St. Jacques* or St. James or pilgrim's shells.

Scallops are the only bivalve molluscs capable of swimming and they move around from the low-tide mark to about 300 feet down. Where the upper and lower shell halves meet, the shell flares out in "wings". The shells open and close by a large adductor muscle, the part of the scallop we eat.

Scallops are primarily harvested by dredging. Once out of the water, they lose moisture quickly and die. Consequently, they are usually shucked on board the ships and refrigerated. In a way this is unfortunate, as another edible part of the scallop, the delicate and delicious pink roe, is most often thrown overboard because it is too perishable to bring ashore.

The sea scallop, *placopecten magellanicus*, found off the south coast of the island and on the southern Grand Banks, is the most commercially important scallop in Newfoundland. It can grow to eight inches in diameter with the adductor muscle sometimes reaching up to two inches across.

The bay scallop, *chlamys islandica*, or Icelandic scallop, is found in bays and estuaries on Newfoundland's south coast. It reaches a maximum size of about four inches in diameter with the adductor muscle about one-half inch across. The bay scallop shell is similar in shape to that of the sea scallop, except that it is smaller, more grooved, with edges that are more serrated.

Raw scallop meat is usually creamy white in colour, although sometimes it can be tinged with orange because of the food the scallop eats. Scallops have a distinct, sweet smell when they are fresh. They freeze well and are adaptable to many cooking methods.

Always take care not to overcook scallops because they toughen easily. As soon as they lose their translucence and turn opaque, they are done.

SCALLOP PUFFS
40 HORS D'OEUVRES

It's hard to stop at one or two of these fantastic little bites. Unless you have a large oven, you will probably have to make them in two batches.

- ½ pound sea scallops, or bay scallops
- ¼ cup mayonnaise
- ¼ cup freshly grated gruyère cheese
- ½ teaspoon prepared Dijon mustard
- 1 teaspoon freshly squeezed lemon juice
- 1 tablespoon finely chopped fresh parsley leaves
- Salt
- Freshly ground black pepper
- 1 large egg white
- 10 large ½-inch thick slices homemade-type white bread, crusts discarded

Preheat the broiler and set a rack about 6 inches from the heat.

In a saucepan, combine the scallops with enough lightly salted water to cover them completely. Bring the water to a simmer, and cook the scallops, maintaining the heat at a slow simmer, for 5 minutes for sea scallops or about 3 minutes for bay scallops. Drain the scallops well.

If using sea scallops, chop them coarsely. If using bay scallops, cut them in half.

In a medium-sized bowl, whisk together the mayonnaise, cheese, mustard, lemon juice and parsley. Stir in the scallops. Season the mixture to taste with salt and pepper. In a small bowl, beat the egg white until it forms stiff peaks and fold it into the scallop mixture gently, but thoroughly.

Using a 2-inch round cookie cutter, cut 4 rounds from each slice of bread. Place the bread rounds about 1 inch apart on 2 large baking sheets. Toast the bread under the broiler, turning the rounds once, just until the bread rounds are a light golden on both sides. Remove the baking sheets from the oven. Top each bread round with a heaping teaspoon of the scallop mixture, spreading it to the edges. Broil the puffs about 6 inches from the heat for 1 to 2 minutes, or until the toppings are bubbling and lightly golden. Serve at once.

Scallops with Lemon-Mustard Sauce

4 Servings

- 1½ pounds sea scallops, patted dry
- Salt
- Freshly ground black pepper
- ¼ cup all-purpose flour
- 1 tablespoon olive oil
- 2 tablespoons unsalted butter
- 1 small garlic clove, minced
- 2 tablespoons freshly squeezed lemon juice
- ¼ cup dry white wine
- 1 tablespoon prepared Dijon mustard
- ¼ cup heavy cream

Serve these scallops with pasta, mashed potatoes or, for a different and delicious twist, over thick slices of toasted French bread.

Dry the scallops well and sprinkle them lightly with salt and pepper. Place the flour on a plate or in a shallow dish. Dip the scallops, a few at a time, into the flour and shake them in a sieve to remove all but a light dusting of flour.

In a large heavy frying pan, heat the oil and butter over moderately low heat. Add the minced garlic and cook it, stirring frequently, for a minute or two. Do not let it brown. Raise the heat to moderately high. Add half the scallops and sear them quickly for 1 to 2 minutes on each side, or until they are golden brown and just cooked through. Transfer the scallops with a slotted spoon to a small heated platter, covered loosely and keep them warm. Repeat with the remaining scallops.

Add the lemon juice and white wine to the frying pan. Bring the mixture to a boil, stirring and scraping up any browned bits. Boil until the mixture is slightly reduced. Whisk in the mustard and the cream and continue whisking about 2 minutes until the sauce simmers and thickens. Taste and adjust the seasonings.

Divide the scallops among 4 heated plates. Spoon some of the sauce over each serving of scallops. Serve immediately.

Sea Scallops with Garlic Butter

6 Servings

- 3 large garlic cloves, put through a garlic press or finely minced
- ½ teaspoon salt, plus more to taste
- ¼ cup unsalted butter, softened
- 2 tablespoons finely chopped fresh parsley leaves
- 1 teaspoon freshly squeezed lemon juice
- 2 pounds whole sea scallops
- ½ cup all-purpose flour, seasoned with salt and white pepper
- 3 tablespoons unsalted butter
- 2 tablespoons vegetable oil
- Lemon wedges

A friend's husband dives for scallops near their home on Newfoundland's east coast. When she gives me really fresh scallops, this is one of my favourite ways to prepare them.

Try to find the best garlic available and if there's a bitter green sprout, remove it.

In a mortar or a small bowl, sprinkle the garlic with the ½ teaspoon of salt. Let the mixture sit for 10 minutes. Using a pestle, or the back of a small spoon, mash the salt and garlic together until they form a smooth paste. Stir in the ¼ cup of softened butter, the parsley and lemon juice and beat the ingredients together until they are well combined. Taste and adjust the seasonings. Set the mixture aside at room temperature.

Dry the scallops well. Place the seasoned flour on a plate or in a shallow dish. Dip the scallops, a few at a time, into the seasoned flour and shake them in a sieve to remove all but a light dusting of flour.

In a large non-stick frying pan, heat the 3 tablespoons of butter and the oil over moderately high heat until the foam begins to subside and the fat is very hot but not smoking. Add half the scallops and sear them quickly for 1 to 2 minutes on each side, or until they are golden brown and just cooked through. With a slotted spoon, transfer the scallops to a small platter, loosely cover them and keep them warm. Repeat with the remaining scallops.

Divide the scallops among 4 heated plates. Divide the garlic butter and spoon some of it over each serving of scallops. Garnish each serving with lemon wedges and serve while the scallops are still hot and the garlic butter is just beginning to melt.

COQUILLES SAINT-JACQUES
SERVING

This is one of my all-time favourite recipes for scallops.

- 1½ cups basic fish stock, or shellfish stock (see recipe index)
- 1½ cups dry white wine
- 2 pounds whole bay scallops, or quartered sea scallops
- ¾ pound small white mushrooms, cut into quarters
- 5 tablespoons unsalted butter
- 5 tablespoons all-purpose flour
- ¾ cup milk, heated
- 2 egg yolks
- ¼ to ½ cup heavy cream
- Salt and white pepper
- Lemon juice
- ½ cup grated gruyère cheese

Preheat the oven to 375°F. Butter 6 large scallop shells or 6 4-inch shallow baking dishes and set them on a large baking sheet.

In a heavy non-reactive 3- to 4-quart saucepan, bring the stock and white wine to a boil over high heat. Reduce the heat and simmer, uncovered, for 5 minutes. Add the scallops and mushrooms. Cover the saucepan and simmer the mixture gently for 5 minutes longer. With a slotted spoon, transfer the scallops and mushrooms to a large bowl and set them aside. Quickly boil down the remaining stock to reduce it to 1 cup. Keep the stock warm.

In a heavy non-reactive saucepan, melt the butter over moderately low heat. Add the flour and, stirring constantly, cook it for 2 minutes. Do not let it brown. Remove the pan from the heat and stir in the hot stock and heated milk. Return the mixture to high heat and, whisking constantly, cook it until it comes to a boil and is thickened. Remove the sauce from the heat.

In a small bowl, mix the egg yolks with ¼ cup of cream. Stir 3 tablespoons of the hot sauce into the egg-yolk mixture. Then pour the egg-yolk mixture back into the remaining sauce. Bring the sauce to a boil over moderate heat, whisking constantly, until it will coat a spoon thickly. If you think it is too thick, thin it out with a little more cream. Season the sauce to taste with salt, white pepper and drops of lemon juice.

Pour half the sauce into the bowl with the scallops and mushrooms, stirring gently to coat. Divide the scallop-mushroom mixture among the scallop shells or baking dishes and mask with the remaining sauce. Sprinkle the cheese evenly over the top. Bake the scallops in the top third of the oven for 10 to 15 minutes, or until the sauce begins to bubble. If desired, turn on the broiler for 1 to 2 minutes to brown the tops lightly. Serve immediately.

SEARED SCALLOPS WITH TOMATOES AND HERBS

4 SERVINGS

I love to prepare this dish when I have fresh thyme and basil growing in my garden.

- 2 tablespoons olive oil
- 2 tablespoons unsalted butter
- 1½ pounds large sea scallops, patted dry
- 3 large garlic cloves, minced
- 2 medium-sized tomatoes, seeded and diced
- 1 teaspoon fresh thyme leaves, or ½ teaspoon dried thyme
- Salt and freshly ground black pepper
- ¼ cup fresh basil leaves, chopped
- Lemon wedges

In a large non-stick frying pan, heat the olive oil and butter over moderately high heat until the foam begins to subside and the fat is very hot but not smoking. Add half the scallops and sear them quickly for 1 to 2 minutes on each side, or until they are golden brown and just cooked through. Transfer the scallops with a slotted spoon to a small platter, cover them loosely and keep them warm. Repeat with the remaining scallops, adding a little extra oil and butter if necessary.

Add the garlic to the frying pan and cook it over moderate heat, stirring frequently, until it is pale golden. Add the tomato and thyme and cook the mixture for about 1 minute. Season the tomato mixture to taste with salt and pepper.

Divide the scallops among 4 heated plates. Spoon the tomato mixture over the scallops and sprinkle each serving with an equal amount of the chopped basil. Garnish each serving with lemon wedges.

SEA TROUT

My husband enjoys angling for trout immensely and he often brings home very fresh, often live, specimens. The trout species he catches depends on the season and the location, but I love to cook and eat them all.

Four main species of sea-run trout live in Newfoundland waters. Two are native and two have been introduced. All four species belong to the family of fishes known as *salmonidae*, which also includes salmon. Like Atlantic salmon, migration to the sea is part of the life cycle of these trout.

Arctic char, *salvelinus alpinus*, are common to Labrador, but were not discovered near the island of Newfoundland until 1949. Their magnificent colouring, fighting spirit and delicious meat make them a highly desirable sport fish. There are two groups of char, freshwater (or land-locked) and sea-run. The sea-run fish are larger, commonly weighing five to ten pounds.

Brook trout, *salvelinus fontinalis*, sometimes called mud trout, speckled trout or brook char, are native to Newfoundland and Labrador. While some brook trout remain in cool lakes and streams, many populations migrate to the sea. Brook trout are considered large if they weigh two pounds.

Since being introduced from Europe to Newfoundland waters on the Avalon Peninsula in the late 1800s, the brown trout, *salmo trutta*, has flourished. Now rivers in the city of St. John's boast the highest population density of brown trout almost anywhere in the world. Angled brown trout of ten pounds are not rare and fish larger than twenty pounds have been caught.

The brilliantly coloured steelhead trout, *oncorhynchus mykiss*, is actually a rainbow trout that has spent part of its life in the ocean. Rainbow trout, *salmo gairdneri*, were introduced to Newfoundland in the 1880s. The average size of these trout is one to two pounds, but fish more than twice that size are not unusual.

Hybrids of all these trout have occurred, some naturally, others crossbred selectively.

All trout have firm-textured delicious meat, fairly high in fat. The colour ranges from pale to very deep pink, depending on the species, environment, diet and size. Generally, small trout are best cooked quickly by grilling, deep-frying or pan-frying. Larger trout, if left whole, are better suited to baking or poaching. All sizes of trout are easily boned before cooking.

TROUTING CAMP BREAKFAST

6 SERVINGS

- ½ pound bacon
- 1 cup all-purpose flour, or cornmeal
- ½ teaspoon salt
- Pepper
- 6 whole trout, 9 to 12 inches in length, cleaned and heads removed, but with tails left on
- Thick slices of home-style bread, toasted over the campfire
- Partridgeberry jam or orange marmalade

Many Newfoundlanders and Labradorians like to spend their leisure time "troutin'", often camping out near their favourite stream or pond. This hearty breakfast for hungry trouters, who are usually up very early in the morning when the fishing is thought to be best.

You could make this at home, of course, but it always seems to taste better when cooked and eaten outdoors. Cups of hot strong tea are the usual accompanying beverage.

Over an open fire or on a camp stove, and using a large heavy frying pan, preferably cast iron, fry the bacon until it is very crisp and brown, turning the strips occasionally. With tongs or a fork, remove the bacon to paper towels and let it drain.

Meanwhile, on a plate or in a paper or plastic bag, mix together the flour or cornmeal, the salt and a few pinches of pepper. Dredge the trout in the flour or cornmeal mixture and shake off the excess.

Over moderately high heat, add the coated trout to the bacon fat remaining in the pan. Fry the trout for 4 or 5 minutes on each side, or until they are well browned and the coating is crispy.

Serve the trout with the bacon, toast and jam or marmalade.

Trout with Cucumber and Yogurt

4 Servings

- 1 large cucumber, peeled, seeded and sliced into thin rounds
- 1 tablespoon chopped fresh dill
- 1 tablespoon freshly squeezed lemon juice
- Salt
- Freshly ground black pepper
- 1 cup unflavoured yogurt
- 1 teaspoon finely grated lemon peel
- 2 tablespoons unsalted butter, melted
- 4 6-ounce trout fillets, with skin

This is a delicate and summery main course, which goes well with rice or a carefully seasoned warm potato salad on the side. If purchasing trout fillets, look for those with skin, or fillet whole trout yourself.

Preheat the oven to 375°F.

In a large bowl, combine the cucumber, 1½ teaspoons of the dill and 1½ teaspoons of the lemon juice. Toss the mixture together lightly and season to taste with salt and pepper. In a small bowl, combine the yogurt, lemon peel and remaining lemon juice. Stir to blend.

Brush a baking sheet with a little of the melted butter. Arrange the trout fillets, skin side down, on the prepared sheet. Brush the top of the fillets with the remaining butter. Bake the trout fillets for about 12 minutes, or until they are just opaque in the centre.

Divide the cucumber mixture among 4 plates. Using a spatula, place the trout fillets on top of the cucumbers. Spoon the yogurt sauce over the trout. Sprinkle each serving with a little of the remaining dill.

BAKED TROUT WITH MUSHROOMS

6 SERVINGS

My husband John loves to fish for trout. On many occasions, the trout have been so fresh that they tasted as if they'd jumped straight from the river into my pan. This is a wonderful recipe for really fresh trout.

- 2 tablespoons olive oil
- ¼ pound bacon, finely chopped
- 1 pound thinly sliced mushrooms
- 1½ cups finely chopped onion
- ½ cup finely chopped celery
- ¼ cup finely chopped fresh parsley
- 1 teaspoon dried thyme
- Salt
- Freshly ground black pepper
- 6 whole trout, about 12 ounces each, cleaned and heads removed, but with tails left on
- 2 tablespoons freshly squeezed lemon juice
- ¼ cup butter, melted

In a large heavy frying pan, heat the olive oil over moderate heat. Add the bacon and sauté, stirring occasionally, until the bacon is crisp and brown and has rendered most of its fat. Using a slotted spoon, remove the bacon from the pan and set it aside to drain on paper towels. To the fat remaining in the pan, add the mushrooms, onion, celery, parsley and thyme. Cook the mixture, stirring frequently, until the mushrooms are browned and almost all the liquid in the pan has evaporated. This will take about 15 minutes. Remove the mixture from the heat and stir in the reserved bacon. Season the mixture to taste with salt and pepper. Let the mixture cool to room temperature.

Preheat the oven to 350°F. Grease a large baking sheet.

Open up the trout and drizzle the cavities evenly with the lemon juice. Sprinkle the insides lightly with salt and pepper. Spoon the mushroom mixture into the cavity of each fish, dividing it equally. Press the sides of the fish together to enclose the filling. If necessary, use small skewers or toothpicks to hold the sides together.

Place the stuffed fish on the prepared sheet. Brush the fish all over with the melted butter.

Bake the trout for about 30 minutes, or until cooked through. Transfer the trout to heated plates and serve immediately.

BAKED TROUT WITH GARLIC CREAM
4 SERVINGS

- 2 whole heads very fresh garlic, cloves separated and peeled
- About ¼ cup olive oil
- Salt
- Freshly ground black pepper
- 4 whole trout, about 12 ounces each, cleaned and heads removed, but with tails left on
- Lemon wedges

This is a recipe I concocted almost by accident when my husband brought home freshly caught trout and I had some garlic cream left over from grilling eggplant. Now this simple preparation has become one of our favourite ways to cook trout.

In a small saucepan, cook the garlic cloves in salted water at a light boil for 15 minutes, or until they are very tender. Drain them and push them through a fine sieve into a small bowl. Gradually stir in enough olive oil to loosen the mixture to a spreading consistency. Season the mixture with salt and pepper to taste.

Preheat the oven to 400°F. Grease a large baking sheet.

Open up the trout and spread a little of the garlic cream inside the cavities. Place the fish on the prepared sheet. Spread the remaining garlic cream all over the outside of the fish.

Bake the trout for about 20 minutes, or until cooked through. Transfer the trout to heated plates and serve immediately garnished with the lemon wedges.

BLUE TROUT
6 SERVINGS

- 2 cups white vinegar
- 6 cups water
- 1 medium-sized carrot, coarsely chopped
- 1 stalk celery, coarsely chopped
- 1 onion, coarsely chopped
- 1 large clove garlic, chopped
- 1 teaspoon salt
- 10 whole black peppercorns
- 3 whole cloves
- 6 live trout, 10 to 12 inches in length
- ½ cup melted butter mixed with 1 tablespoon freshly squeezed
- lemon juice (optional)
- ½ cup mayonnaise, preferably homemade (optional)

This is an unusual way to cook trout and makes for a dramatic presentation because the trout really do turn blue. Do not attempt this recipe unless you start with live trout, and do not wash the trout because the natural protective film must be present to make the recipe work.

The trout may be served hot with melted butter and lemon juice, or cold with mayonnaise.

In a large non-reactive pot, at least 12 inches in diameter, combine the vinegar, water, carrot, celery, onion, garlic, salt, peppercorns and cloves. Bring the mixture to a simmer.

Kill the trout and gut them, handling them as little as possible. Do not wash them. Leave the heads and tails intact. Using tongs so as not to disturb the protective coating, quickly immerse the trout in the simmering liquid. When all the trout are immersed, bring the mixture to a rapid boil. Immediately remove the pot from the heat, cover it and let it stand for 15 minutes.

Carefully remove the trout from the pot and drain them on paper towels. Discard the liquid.

Serve the trout hot with melted butter and lemon, or chill and serve them cold with mayonnaise.

STEELHEAD TROUT WITH BASIL SAUCE
4 SERVINGS

- 1 cup finely chopped fresh basil leaves
- ½ cup finely chopped fresh parsley leaves
- 2 large cloves garlic, chopped
- 6 tablespoons extra-virgin olive oil
- 2 tablespoons water
- 3 tablespoons freshly squeezed lemon juice
- Salt
- Freshly ground black pepper
- 4 6-ounce steelhead trout fillets, with skin
- 1 large lemon, cut lengthwise into 8 wedges

A potato gratin and baked or broiled tomatoes make terrific accompaniments to this easy, yet elegant dish.

In a food processor or blender, pulse together the basil, parsley and garlic. Add 4 tablespoons of the olive oil and continue to pulse until the mixture is puréed to a smooth paste. Blend in the water and the lemon juice. Taste for seasoning and add salt and freshly ground black pepper. If the basil sauce seems too thick, thin it with a little more water. Transfer the sauce to a small bowl and set it aside at room temperature.

Preheat the broiler and set an oven rack about 6 inches from the heat source.

Arrange the trout fillets, skin sides down, on an oiled baking sheet. Brush the fillets with the remaining 2 tablespoons of olive oil, sprinkle them evenly with the remaining tablespoon of lemon juice and season them with salt and pepper.

Broil the trout fillets, without turning them, for about 7 minutes, or until they are just cooked through and flake easily when prodded with a fork, about 7 minutes.

Place a large spoonful of the basil sauce on each of four heated plates. Top the sauce with the trout fillets and garnish each serving with 2 lemon wedges.

CHAR IN PARCHMENT
4 SERVINGS

- 3 tablespoons unsalted butter, softened
- 1 large leek, white and pale green parts only, cut into julienne (matchstick-sized pieces), or substitute 1 medium-sized onion, diced small
- 1 clove garlic, mashed
- 1 medium-sized carrot, cut into julienne
- 2 stalks celery, cut into julienne
- 1 large ripe tomato, peeled and cut into ¼-inch dice
- 1 tablespoon finely chopped fresh parsley leaves
- ½ teaspoon dried tarragon
- ½ teaspoon salt
- ¼ teaspoon freshly ground black pepper
- ½ cup dry white wine
- 4 char fillets, each about 5 ounces

Almost any fish is wonderful cooked this way and we often enjoy cod fillets using the same recipe.

Bring the sealed packages to the table so that each diner can slit one open and inhale the wonderful heady vapours. Parchment paper is generally available in kitchen shops, hardware stores and some supermarkets.

In a heavy 8- to 10-inch frying pan, melt 2 tablespoons of the butter over moderate heat. When the foam subsides, add the leek or onion, garlic, carrot and celery and cook, stirring, for about 5 minutes, or until the vegetables are soft but not brown. Stir in the tomato, parsley, tarragon, salt, pepper and white wine and cook, stirring, for about 5 minutes longer, or until most of the liquid has evaporated. Taste for seasoning. Remove the vegetable mixture from the heat and set it aside.

Preheat the oven to 400°F. Use the remaining tablespoon of butter to grease 4 12-inch squares of parchment paper.

Arrange a char fillet on each square of parchment. Divide the vegetable mixture evenly and spread it over the fish. Bring up the sides of the paper and fold them together to create an airtight package. Place the packages on a large baking sheet and bake for 20 minutes. The parchment paper will turn a golden brown.

As soon as it is cooked, serve the char in the parchment to be opened at the table.

SEAL

No book about Newfoundland and Labrador seafood would be complete without the inclusion of seals, marine mammals harvested long before Europeans fished or settled here.

In the early eighteenth century, English settlers on the northeast coast of Newfoundland began hunting seals. Some were caught using nets in the spring when the ice brought the whelping herd within walking distance from shore. Others were hunted later in the season using small boats and guns. The pelts were sold on the European market, but the oil was of greater value and large quantities of it were shipped back to England to be used as fuel for lamps, lubricating and cooking oil, for processing leather and as a soap ingredient. Newfoundlanders ate the meat. Almost nothing was wasted.

By the late eighteenth century, much larger ships were being used and the method of harvesting seals involved sailing to the great expanses of ice that surround the Newfoundland and Labrador coasts in the spring. Ships stopped near the ice floes and the crews of "swilers", as they were called, combed the ice on foot in search of seal herds. Then a long wooden gaff was used to kill the seals. Later, rifles were used.

Much history, folklore and myth surrounds the history of the seal hunt. Every year, for generations, poor and ill-clad Newfoundland fishermen went "to the ice" in the hope of earning a little extra money for their families. There were numerous tragedies. The worst of these, in 1914, is well documented in Cassie Brown's compelling book *Death on the Ice*.

Now the Canadian government regulates the seal hunt and quotas are set. Although harp seals (*phoca groenlandica*) are the focus of the commercial hunt, a smaller number of hood seals (*cystophora cristata*) are commercially hunted each year. Other species of seals are also harvested in non-commercial hunts.

Seal meat is dark and dense and rich in protein and iron. All traces of fat, which has an unpleasant flavour, must be removed before cooking.

It's probably an acquired taste, but properly prepared seal meat can be delicious. My mother often cooked—and still cooks—a rib roast of seal, but, by far, the most popular seal dish in Newfoundland and Labrador is flipper pie, the only recipe for seal meat I've given here.

SEAL FLIPPER PIE

6 SERVINGS

This makes a hearty meal, well loved by many Newfoundlanders.

- 2 seal flippers, skinned
- 2 tablespoons baking soda
- 2¼ cups all-purpose flour
- 1 teaspoon salt
- Freshly ground black pepper
- 1 coarsely chopped onion
- 3 medium-sized carrots, cut into ½-inch dice
- 1 small turnip, cut into ½-inch dice
- 3 medium-sized boiling potatoes, cut into ½-inch dice
- 2 teaspoons baking powder
- ½ cup cold unsalted butter, cut into small bits
- ¼ to ½ cup cold milk

With the aid of a sharp knife and a stiff-bristled brush, remove as much of the surface fat as you can from the flippers. In a large bowl, dissolve the baking soda in enough cold water to cover the flippers. Soak the flippers for about 1 hour, or until the remaining fat turns white. Drain the flippers and, using the knife and brush, remove the remaining fat. With a sharp knife, remove the meat from the bones and cut it into 1-inch cubes.

Preheat the oven to 450°F. Mix together ¼ cup of the flour with ½ teaspoon of salt and a generous grinding of pepper. Dredge the flipper pieces in the flour mixture until they are evenly coated.

In a 3-quart baking dish, combine the flipper pieces with the chopped onion and bake, uncovered, for 5 minutes. Stir up the ingredients and bake for 5 minutes longer. (This will brown the meat.) Reduce the oven temperature to 350°F. Add enough water to just cover the meat, cover the dish and bake for 2½ hours. Remove the baking dish from the oven and stir in the carrots, turnip and potatoes. Recover the baking dish and return it to the oven. Bake 40 minutes longer, or until the meat and vegetables are tender.

Meanwhile, in a large bowl, stir together the remaining 2 cups of flour, the remaining ½ teaspoon of salt and the baking powder. With a pastry blender or your fingertips, blend in the butter until the mixture resembles coarse meal. Gradually mix in enough cold milk to form a soft, but workable, dough. Roll out the dough to the approximate size of the baking dish.

Remove the baking dish from the oven and increase the temperature to 400°F. Cover the meat and vegetables with the pastry, trimming it to fit the dish. Bake the pie for 30 minutes, or until golden. Serve it from the dish.

SHARK

Many people are surprised to learn that there are sharks in Newfoundland waters, but, in fact, a number of shark species are found here. While none of these are considered man-eating, all sharks are potentially dangerous. They have large jaws with rows of sharp teeth and can whip their tails around to inflict serious wounds with their long and spiny fins.

At present there is no directed commercial shark fishery in Newfoundland waters, but there is a fishery outside the two-hundred-mile limit. Until the 1970s, the dogfish shark, *squalus acanthias*, a small shark also known as the spiny dogfish or cod shark, was found in waters all around Newfoundland and Labrador. It was most populous off the south coast of the island, where there was a sizable commercial fishery for the species. This shark is no longer abundant, a fact that may be attributed to its migratory nature rather than over-fishing, and is no longer commercially fished.

Since the 1970s, the main shark species taken from Newfoundland waters, generally as by-catch, are the blue shark, *prionace glauca*, the mako shark, *isurus oxyrinchus*, and the porbeagle shark, *lamna nasus*.

Sharks are primitive fish with a cartilage, rather than bone, skeleton, which enables them to glide quickly to a food source or dive to the bottom and rocket to the surface in a moment. All sharks are voracious predators. Their body skin is rough and leathery. They bear their young live.

Sharks have a primitive body-fluid control system and retain urea to keep their fluids at the same density as seawater. For this reason, they must be soaked to rid the flesh of a strong ammonia taste and odour. If the shark has been properly handled before marketing, however, soaking at home should not be necessary.

Mako shark, in particular, is prized as food fish and can be found in many markets, but other shark is also often available. Generally, the smaller the shark, the more tender the meat. Shark meat is firm with a rich, but mild flavour. After purchasing, cook it as soon as possible. Freezing alters the texture.

Shark takes well to marinating, but not for too long. It can be baked, poached or fried and, because it is dense and firm, it's ideal for grilling. Take care not to overcook shark because it dries out easily.

SHARK STEW

4 SERVINGS

Thick slices of crusty bread to sop up the flavourful juices are a must with this easy-to-make stew.

- 3 tablespoons olive oil
- 1 cup finely chopped onions
- 3 large garlic cloves, chopped
- 1 cup finely chopped fresh parsley
- ½ teaspoon dried oregano
- 1 large vine-ripened tomato, cored, seeded and coarsely chopped
- 2 cups basic fish stock (see recipe index)
- ½ cup dry white wine
- 2 pounds skinless, boneless shark meat, cut into 2-inch pieces
- Salt
- Freshly ground black pepper

In a large heavy pot, heat the olive over moderate heat. Add the chopped onion and garlic and sauté, stirring for about 5 minutes, or until the vegetables are soft but not brown. Add the parsley and oregano and stir for about 2 minutes. Add the tomato and cook 2 minutes longer. Stir in the fish stock and white wine and simmer for about 10 minutes longer, or until the mixture is slightly reduced. Add the shark pieces and continue to simmer, uncovered, stirring occasionally, until the fish is cooked through, about 12 minutes.

Season the stew to taste with salt and pepper. Ladle it into heated bowls and serve.

ASIAN-STYLE GRILLED SHARK
4 SERVINGS

- ½ cup soy sauce
- 2 tablespoons Asian sesame oil
- 1 teaspoon minced fresh ginger root
- 3 tablespoons sugar
- 1 tablespoon sesame seeds
- 3 cloves garlic, minced
- ¼ teaspoon salt
- ½ teaspoon freshly ground black pepper
- 1½ pounds shark steak, at least 1 inch thick, cut into 4 portions
- Vegetable oil for brushing grill
- Fresh cilantro leaves for garnish

The aromatic marinade adds wonderful flavour to the shark meat. Do not marinate the shark for longer than 2 hours, however, as the enzymes in the ginger can over-tenderize the fish and make it mushy.

In a large shallow bowl, combine the soy sauce, sesame oil, ginger, sugar, sesame seeds, garlic, salt and pepper. Stir the ingredients to combine well. Add the pieces of shark and turn them to coat. Cover the bowl with plastic wrap and refrigerate. Let the shark marinate for 1 to 2 hours, but no longer, turning it occasionally.

Preheat a barbecue grill to moderately high heat and brush it lightly with vegetable oil.

Drain the shark pieces and discard the marinade. (Some of the sesame seeds may cling to the fish pieces. You may brush them off or leave them in place.) Grill the shark for about 4 minutes on each side, or until just cooked through.

Serve on heated plates garnished with cilantro leaves.

Shark with Honey Sauce

4 Servings

- 1½ pounds shark meat, about 1 inch thick, cut into serving-sized pieces
- 1½ teaspoons ground cumin
- ½ teaspoon salt
- ¼ teaspoon freshly ground black pepper
- ½ teaspoon peanut oil, or sunflower oil
- ½ cup dry white wine
- ½ teaspoon chicken bouillon granules
- ¼ cup freshly squeezed lime juice
- 2 tablespoons honey
- 1 teaspoon cornstarch stirred together with 1 tablespoon water

The two-step method of searing and then roasting the shark makes it very succulent. Rice is an excellent accompaniment to this dish, but you might like to try couscous, a now widely available small North African pasta.

Preheat the oven to 500°F.

Pat the shark pieces dry. In a small bowl, combine the cumin, salt and pepper. Sprinkle the spice mixture evenly on both sides of the shark pieces and, using your fingertips, gently massage it into the fish.

In a large heavy oven-proof frying pan (preferably a cast-iron pan), heat the oil over high heat until it is hot but not smoking. Lay the fish pieces in the pan and sear them until they are well browned on one side, about 5 minutes. Turn the fish over and place the frying pan in the hot oven. Roast the shark until it is just cooked through, about 10 minutes.

Meanwhile, in a small saucepan, whisk together the wine, chicken bouillon granules and lime juice. Bring the mixture to a simmer. Stir in the honey and simmer until it dissolves. Stir the cornstarch-and-water mixture to combine and whisk it into the sauce. Continue to cook, whisking, until the sauce is slightly thickened, 4 to 5 minutes.

Place the shark on warm plates and spoon the honey sauce over and around the fish.

SHRIMP

The terms "shrimp", "prawns" and "scampi" can be confusing. Sometimes they are used interchangeably, but "prawn" usually refers to the larger freshwater or saltwater shrimp. To add to the confusion, many restaurants call those very same shrimp "scampi" when they are prepared with butter and garlic. Basically, however, all shrimp can be divided into three categories: freshwater shrimp, warm-water or southern shrimp, and coldwater or northern shrimp.

The shrimp caught in Newfoundland waters, primarily off the coast of Labrador, are northern coldwater shrimp, *pandalus borealis*. They live in areas where the ocean floor is soft and muddy and where bottom temperatures are only a few degrees above freezing. During the day, the shrimp spend much of their time resting and feeding on or near the ocean floor. At night, most of them migrate vertically in the water column, feeding on a variety of tiny sea creatures and plankton. They are prey to many other species, including cod, halibut, skate, wolf fish and seals.

Coldwater shrimp have bright, reddish-pink shells, both raw and cooked. The meat is pinker, softer and more intensely flavoured than that of warm-water shrimp. A coldwater shrimp is much smaller on average than its warm-water cousins. It does not need to have the sand vein, which runs along its back, removed before eating because it is so small.

All varieties of shrimp are usually sold by count per pound. Still in their shells, the average count for commercially caught coldwater shrimp is about fifty. Shrimp are marketed in a variety of ways, fresh or frozen, raw or cooked, with or without shells. Whenever possible, I prefer to buy raw shrimp in their shells and cook them that way. They are easier to peel after cooking and the shrimp will retain their juices better. The tiny coldwater shrimp are particularly tedious to shell raw because there are so many of them per pound.

Many cooking methods can be used for shrimp. They may be poached, sautéed or grilled and served either hot or cold. They should never be overcooked because they toughen easily. Perfect shrimp should be cooked just to the point where the flesh turns from translucent to opaque.

Toasted Shrimp Rolls
28 Hors d'Oeuvres

These easy hors d'oeuvres can be made ahead of time and popped into the oven just before serving. They're always very popular, so you might even want to double the recipe.

- 1 pound small shrimp, shelled and deveined
- ¼ cup freshly grated sharp cheddar cheese
- 2 tablespoons freshly grated parmesan cheese
- ¼ cup heavy cream
- 1 tablespoon medium-dry sherry
- 2 tablespoons minced green onions
- 14 slices thin white sandwich bread, crusts trimmed and discarded
- ¼ cup butter, melted
- Cocktail sauce (see recipe index)

Bring a large saucepan full of lightly salted water to a boil. Plunge in the shrimp. Reduce the heat to a slow simmer and simmer the shrimp until they are just cooked through, 1 to 2 minutes. Drain the shrimp in a colander and rinse them under cold water. Pat the shrimp dry and chop them finely.

In a medium-sized bowl, stir together the shrimp, cheeses, cream, sherry, and green onions. Set the mixture aside.

Using a rolling pin, flatten each bread slice as thinly as possible. Put about 2 tablespoons of the shrimp mixture on each bread slice and roll it up tightly. With a sharp knife, cut each roll in half crosswise. Put the rolls, seam sides down, on a lightly greased baking sheet and brush them all over with the melted butter. Chill the rolls, covered loosely, at least 1 hour and up to 4 hours.

Preheat the oven to 425°F.

Bake the shrimp rolls until toasted golden, about 12 minutes. Serve the shrimp rolls hot with cocktail sauce for dipping.

CURRIED SHRIMP WITH MARMALADE DIP

A sweet-and-spicy dip provides the perfect foil for crispy baked shrimp.

- 1 tablespoon vegetable oil
- 1 pound medium to large shrimp, shelled and deveined
- ¾ cup dry bread crumbs
- 1 teaspoon curry powder
- ¼ teaspoon salt
- 1 egg
- 1 tablespoon water
- 3 tablespoons melted unsalted butter
- 3 tablespoons orange marmalade
- 1 tablespoon ginger marmalade
- 1 small clove garlic, minced
- 1 teaspoon cornstarch dissolved in 3 tablespoons soy sauce

Preheat the oven to 500°F. Grease a large baking sheet with the tablespoon of vegetable oil.

Dry the shrimp well. In a shallow bowl, combine the bread crumbs, curry powder and salt. In a small bowl, beat the egg together with the tablespoon of water. Dip each shrimp in the egg mixture and then roll it in the breadcrumb mixture to coat well. Place the shrimp on the baking sheet, spacing them a little apart. Drizzle the shrimp evenly with the melted butter and bake them in the middle of the oven for about 10 minutes, or until they are golden brown and crisp.

While the shrimp are baking, combine the marmalades, garlic and cornstarch-soy mixture in a small saucepan. Stir to mix well. Over moderate heat, cook the mixture until it begins to bubble. Reduce the heat and cook, stirring constantly, until the mixture is thickened and the sauce is translucent.

To serve, spear each shrimp on a cocktail pick or small fork and dip it into the marmalade-soy sauce.

SHRIMP SALAD
4 SERVINGS

Much of the preparation for this refreshingly light luncheon dish can be done beforehand.

- ½ cup mayonnaise, preferably homemade (see recipe index)
- ¼ cup ketchup
- 2 tablespoons cognac, or other good-quality French brandy
- 1 tablespoon freshly squeezed lime juice
- ½ teaspoon sugar
- 1 teaspoon prepared horseradish
- 2 large navel oranges
- 1½ pounds large shrimp, shelled and deveined
- 2 teaspoons extra-virgin olive oil
- ½ teaspoon minced garlic
- 2 large firm, ripe avocados
- 1 head Boston lettuce or butter lettuce, separated into leaves

In a small bowl, stir together the mayonnaise, ketchup, cognac, lime juice, sugar and horseradish. Whisk the sauce until well combined and smooth. (The sauce may be made several hours, or even a day, ahead of time and chilled, covered.)

Working over a bowl, peel and section the oranges, letting the sections drop into the bowl and squeezing in any excess juice from the membranes.

In a large saucepan of simmering salted water, cook the shrimp at a bare simmer just until they are firm, 2 to 4 minutes, depending on their size. Do not overcook. Drain the shrimp in a colander and transfer them to a large bowl. While the shrimp are still warm, add the oil, garlic, and any juice from the orange sections, stirring to coat the shrimp. Let the shrimp cool to room temperature.

Peel the avocados and cut them into ½-inch dice. Fold the orange sections and avocado into the shrimp mixture, stirring the ingredients together gently until just mixed.

Line 4 large salad plates with the lettuce leaves. Divide the shrimp salad among the plates. Spoon the sauce equally over each serving.

Shrimp in Spicy Butter Sauce
Serving

- 3 large cloves garlic, minced
- 1 tablespoon freshly ground black pepper, preferably a coarse grind
- 1 tablespoon Worcestershire sauce
- ¾ teaspoon Tabasco sauce
- ½ teaspoon dried basil
- ½ teaspoon dried summer savory
- ¾ teaspoon salt
- ¾ cup unsalted butter, softened
- 2 tablespoons freshly squeezed lemon juice
- 2 pounds small shrimp in their shells
- 6 green onions, including some of the green tops, finely chopped
- Lemon wedges

If you like your food a bit spicy—yes, a whole tablespoon of black pepper and then some Tabasco sauce—this is one of the most delicious ways to serve small North Atlantic shrimp.

The shrimp are somewhat messy to eat, but they make a wonderful informal supper. Provide plenty of napkins and a large bowl for the discarded shells. Don't forget a big loaf of crusty bread to sop up the sauce.

Preheat the oven to 500°F.

In a medium-sized bowl, stir together the minced garlic, pepper, Worcestershire sauce, Tabasco sauce, basil, savory and salt. Add the butter and, mashing it against the sides of the bowl, beat it until the spices are incorporated well. Beat in the lemon juice to combine. Taste and adjust the seasonings.

Spread the shrimp in a shallow baking dish large enough to hold them in one layer.

Sprinkle the shrimp evenly with the green onions. Drop spoonfuls of the butter mixture evenly over the top of the shrimp. Bake the shrimp, stirring once or twice, just until they are cooked through, about 8 minutes.

Serve the shrimp and sauce in heated deep plates. Garnish with the lemon wedges.

SHRIMP CREOLE
4 SERVINGS

This is a classic and always-popular main course.

- 2 tablespoons olive oil
- 4 large cloves garlic, minced
- 2 medium-sized onions, finely chopped
- 2 stalks celery, finely chopped
- ½ red bell pepper, cut into ½-inch dice
- ½ green bell pepper, cut into ½-inch dice
- 2 cups basic fish stock, or shellfish stock (see recipe index)
- 1 28-ounce can tomatoes, drained and chopped
- 1 teaspoon ground cumin
- ½ teaspoon chili powder
- 1 bay leaf
- ½ teaspoon salt
- ½ teaspoon freshly ground black pepper
- 2 teaspoons Worcestershire sauce
- 1½ pounds shrimp, shelled and deveined
- Cooked rice as an accompaniment

In a large heavy saucepan, heat the olive oil over moderately low heat. Add the garlic, onions, celery, and bell peppers and cook them, stirring occasionally, for about 10 minutes, or until the vegetables are soft but not brown.

Stir in the stock, tomatoes, cumin, chili powder, bay leaf, salt, pepper and Worcestershire sauce. Bring the mixture to a simmer and continue to simmer, uncovered, for about 30 minutes or until thickened.

Stir in the shrimp and cook, covered, over moderate heat, stirring occasionally, until the shrimp are cooked through, about 3 to 5 minutes, depending on their size. Taste and adjust the seasonings.

Spoon a portion of cooked rice into each of 4 heated bowls or deep plates. Ladle the shrimp mixture over the rice.

SKATE

In recent years skate has become remarkably common on restaurant menus, but is not yet so well known to home cooks. This is unfortunate, for it is available in many markets, is delectable and is not difficult to prepare.

The bottom-dwelling kite-shaped skate, a primitive relative of the shark, is found worldwide, both in cold and temperate waters. Skates are generally grey-brown in colour, with flat bodies and short spineless tails. They swim by undulating their fins, or "wings". Like sharks, they have powerful jaws for crushing mollusc and crustacean shells, creatures for which they have a particular fondness.

The smooth skate, *raja senta*, is found mainly in the southern half of Newfoundland waters. The larger thorny skate, *raja radiata*, is found in waters all around Newfoundland and Labrador. A third species, *raja laevis*, commonly called "barndoor" skate, is also present in deep water all around the province. Skate are taken with longlines and gillnets, both as a targeted fishery and as by-catch. They can be harvested throughout the year, but it is often said they are best in winter.

Only the wings of the skate are eaten. They are delicious, with a mildly pronounced flavour similar to scallops. The raw meat has a white or pinkish-white colour that cooks to off-white. Each wing produces two fillets, one from the upper and one from the lower side. These are usually skinned before the fillets are sold.

Because of the striated fan-like wing structure of the wings, skate can have a stringy texture. In markets, skate has usually been aged slightly, but will improve in texture if left to stand refrigerated for a day or so, to firm up and become more delicate.

Skate is adaptable to many recipes and may be sautéed in butter, pan-fried, deep-fried, baked or poached.

SKATE WING WITH VINAIGRETTE SAUCE
4 SERVINGS

A wide pasta, such as fettuccine, makes a great complement to this highly flavoured dish.

- 6 tablespoons olive oil
- 1½ pounds skate-wing fillets, cut into 4 equal portions
- ½ cup coarsely chopped calamata olives, or other brine-cured olives
- ½ cup coarsely chopped drained bottled roasted red pepper
- 3 tablespoons finely chopped fresh parsley leaves, preferably flat-leaf parsley
- 2 tablespoons drained bottled capers, chopped
- 1 tablespoon anchovy paste
- 1 large garlic clove, minced and mashed to a paste with ½ teaspoon salt
- ¼ cup minced green onion, including some of the green tops
- 3 tablespoons red-wine vinegar
- Salt
- Freshly ground black pepper
- Lemon wedges for garnish

In a large heavy frying pan, preferably non-stick, heat 2 tablespoons of the oil over moderately high heat until it is hot but not smoking. Sauté the skate fillets for about 6 to 8 minutes on each side, or until they are cooked through to the centre.

While the skate is cooking, in a bowl, stir together the olives, roasted red pepper, parsley, capers, anchovy paste, garlic paste and green onions. Stir in the vinegar and the remaining 4 tablespoons of olive oil. Season to taste with salt and black pepper.

Transfer the skate fillets to heated plates, spoon the sauce over them, and serve them with the lemon wedges.

Skate with Brown Butter Sauce
4 Servings

A golden brown butter sauce with capers adds intensity to a simple sauté of skate-wing fillets.

- ¼ cup all-purpose flour
- ½ teaspoon salt
- ¼ teaspoon freshly ground black pepper
- 1½ pounds skate-wing fillets, cut into 4 equal portions
- 2 tablespoons olive oil
- ¼ cup unsalted butter
- 1 tablespoon capers, rinsed and drained
- 1 tablespoon white wine vinegar

Spread the flour on a large piece of waxed paper and season it with the salt and pepper. Lightly dredge the fillets on both sides in the flour, shaking off the excess.

In a large heavy frying pan, preferably with a non-stick coating, heat the oil over moderately high heat. When the oil is hot but not smoking, add the fillets. (If it is necessary to do this in two batches, you may have to use a little extra oil.) Sauté the fillets on one side until golden brown, about 3 minutes. Turn them and cook on the other side until golden brown, about 3 minutes more.

Meanwhile, in a small saucepan, bring the butter to a boil over high heat, stirring. When it begins to turn a golden brown, pour in the vinegar and stir in the capers. Remove the sauce from the heat.

When the skate fillets are done, transfer them to a heated platter or heated individual serving plates. Pour a tablespoon or so of the butter sauce over each serving.

Pan-Fried Skate with Pepper Sauce

4 Servings

The pepper here is red bell pepper, but green or yellow peppers may be used. A mixture of different coloured peppers would give the dish even greater eye-appeal.

- 1½ pounds skate-wing fillets, cut into 4 equal portions
- ½ cup milk
- Salt
- Freshly ground black pepper
- ¼ cup all-purpose flour
- 3 tablespoons olive oil, plus extra if needed
- 3 tablespoons butter
- 1 large red bell pepper, seeded and cut into ¼-inch dice
- 2 tablespoons drained capers
- 2 tablespoon finely minced shallots
- 2 tablespoons red wine vinegar
- 3 tablespoons finely chopped parsley
- Lemon wedges for garnish

Place the skate-wing fillets in a dish large enough to hold them in one layer. Pour the milk over them and sprinkle with salt and pepper. Turn the fillets in the milk so they are coated on both sides.

Spread the flour on a large piece of waxed paper. Lightly dredge the fillets on both sides in the flour, shaking off the excess.

In a large heavy frying pan, preferably with a non-stick coating, heat the oil over moderately high heat. When the oil is hot but not smoking, add the fillets. (If it is necessary to do this in two batches, you may have to use a little extra oil.) Sauté the fillets on one side until golden brown, about 3 minutes. Turn them and cook on the other side until golden brown, about 3 minutes more. When the fillets are done, transfer them to a heated platter or heated individual serving plates. Keep the fillets warm in a low oven while you make the sauce.

Wipe out the pan with a paper towel and return it to moderate heat. Add the butter to the pan and let it melt. Add the diced red pepper and, stirring frequently, cook until the pepper is soft and the butter lightly browned. Stir in the capers, shallots, vinegar and parsley. Cook briefly, stirring, just to heat the sauce through. Pour the sauce over the skate-wing fillets, garnish with lemon wedges and serve at once.

SQUID

There's a Newfoundland saying, applied to someone who exhibits unpredictable behaviour, that "you can't tell the mind of a squid". That's because, while a squid can move forward, it has a siphon that takes in and expels water for extremely rapid "jet" propulsion backwards. The siphon also ejects a bluish-black "ink" that helps obscure the squid from its predators.

The squid is an odd-looking creature. Its long body is joined to its head, which has 10 arms sticking out of it. People are often surprised to learn that squid, with no external shells, are related to molluscs such as clams, oysters and scallops. The cellophane-like "pen" that runs through the squid's soft, muscular body, or "mantle", is, in fact, a vestigial shell.

Squid are generally a mixed iridescent colour of milky white and rusty brown. The colour changes rapidly as the squid expands or contracts, going lighter and darker, and acts as camouflage in response to attack.

Squid caught in Newfoundland and Labrador waters are the short-finned species, *illex illecebrosus*. They are usually fished by trapping or by jigging from small boats. Until the early 1970s, squid were pursued largely for bait. However, now an international fishery has developed and squid are processed for export to Japan, the world's foremost consumer of squid, as well as to a number of other countries.

The average weight of commercially caught squid is from one-quarter to just over half a pound. The smaller squid are great for deep-frying; the larger size is perfect for stuffing.

If you can't find fresh squid, the frozen kind are often available in five-pound boxes of squished-together cleaned squid. To prepare a recipe using frozen squid, partially thaw a box in the fridge, pull off as much as you need, reseal the semi-solid block and return it to the freezer. Let the portion to be cooked thaw fully.

Squid meat is snowy white with a somewhat chewy texture that should never be tough. The key to cooking squid is time and temperature. There are two basic techniques. One is to flip them over in a pan on high heat for a few seconds. Small squid or squid slices will be cooked through without becoming tough. The other approach is to simmer them slowly in liquid for a much longer period of time, or until they pass through the tough stage and become tender again.

Deep-Fried Squid with Salad
6 First-Course Servings

Buttermilk gives the squid a light and tender coating.

- 2 cups buttermilk
- 2 cups all-purpose flour
- Salt
- Freshly ground black pepper
- 3 cups vegetable oil for deep frying
- 1½ pounds cleaned squid, bodies cut into ½-inch rings, tentacles left intact
- ¼ cup extra-virgin olive oil
- 1 tablespoon balsamic vinegar
- ½ pound mesclun (mixed baby lettuce greens)
- 12 cherry tomatoes
- 2 lemons, each cut into 6 wedges

Pour the buttermilk into a large bowl. Place the flour in another large bowl. Season the flour with salt and pepper.

Pour the vegetable oil into a deep heavy saucepan or deep fryer. Heat the oil to 375°F on a deep-frying thermometer. Working in small batches of 6 to 8 pieces, dip the squid into the buttermilk, turning them to coat. Remove them from the buttermilk and dredge them in the flour, shaking off the excess. Carefully add the first batch of squid to the oil. Fry the pieces, turning them about to keep them from sticking together, until they are golden brown and crisp, about 1 minute. Using a slotted spoon, transfer the squid to paper towels to drain and keep them warm in

a low oven. Repeat the procedure with the remaining squid, making sure the oil returns to 375°F between each batch.

In a large bowl, stir together the olive oil and balsamic vinegar. Season the mixture to taste with salt and freshly ground pepper. Toss in the lettuce greens and continue to toss until all the leaves are lightly coated with the dressing.

Divide the salad greens among 6 plates. Place the warm squid on top of the greens, dividing it equally. Garnish each plate with 2 cherry tomatoes and 2 lemon wedges.

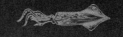

STUFFED SQUID
4 SERVINGS

This is one of my very favourite ways to prepare squid.

- 8 to 10 squid bodies ("tubes") plus some of the tentacles if you have them
- 2 tablespoons olive oil
- 1 small onion, finely chopped
- 3 cloves garlic, finely chopped
- 1 large tomato, peeled, seeded and cut into very small dice
- 1 teaspoon fresh thyme leaves, or ¼ teaspoon dried thyme
- 10 to 12 oil-cured black olives, pits removed and finely chopped

Wash the squid tubes under cold water. Reach inside the tubes with your finger to make sure the cellophane-like "pen" has been removed. Trim off the triangular "fins" with kitchen scissors, making sure not to pierce the tubes. If you have tentacles, finely chop enough to make about ¼ cup.

Heat the oil in a medium-sized frying pan and cook the onion and garlic over low heat for about 5 minutes, or until they are soft but not brown. Add the chopped tentacles, if you have them, the tomato, thyme and olives and cook for about 5 minutes, stirring, or until very soft. Stir in the bread crumbs, lemon peel and parsley. Taste for seasoning and add salt and pepper if needed. Set the mixture aside to cool to room temperature.

Using a pastry or cake-decorating bag with a fairly large tip, fill each squid tube with the stuffing to about 1 inch from the opening. (The squid will shrink and the stuffing will expand as it cooks, so make sure the tubes are not too full or they will burst.) Using a large needle and kitchen string, sew up the top of each tube close to the edge by pulling the needle through two opposite sides and then through the other two sides and tying a knot. Place the filled tubes in a shallow baking dish just large enough to hold them comfortably in one layer. Pour in the wine or combination of wine and fish stock and add enough water if necessary so that the squid are completely covered. The squid may now be refrigerated for several hours until you are ready to cook them.

Preheat the oven to 375° F. Bake the squid for about 1 hour, basting them every 10 minutes or so with the liquid in the baking dish.

When the squid are done, use kitchen scissors to snip off the string. Serve the squid whole with a little liquid from the dish ladled over them.

LINGUINE WITH CALAMARI

4 SERVINGS

- 1 pound dried linguine, preferably black squid-ink linguine
- 1 2-ounce can rolled anchovies with capers, anchovies crushed and oil from the can reserved
- 1 tablespoon olive oil
- 1 pound cleaned squid, bodies cut into ¼-inch rings, tentacles left intact
- 1 whole small head garlic, cloves separated, peeled and coarsely chopped
- ¼ teaspoon dried crushed red pepper
- 1½ cups dry white wine
- 1 cup thinly sliced fresh basil leaves, packed
- Parmesan cheese

Squid are called "calamari" in Italian and you will often see them listed that way on menus, even in non-Italian restaurants. If you can find black squid-ink linguine, it is wonderful in this recipe. If not, use regular white linguine.

In a large pot of boiling salted water, cook the pasta until it is just tender, but still firm to the bite, stirring occasionally. Drain the pasta, reserving ½ cup of the cooking liquid. Return the pasta to the pot and partially cover to keep it warm.

Meanwhile, in a large frying pan over moderate heat, heat the reserved oil from the anchovies along with the tablespoon of olive oil. Add the squid pieces and toss them in the pan just until they just turn opaque, about 1 minute. Add the garlic, crushed red pepper and crushed anchovies with capers and stir for 1 minute longer. Pour in the white wine. Bring the mixture to a boil and boil until the sauce is slightly reduced, about 3 minutes. Stir in the basil leaves.

Add the mixture in the frying pan to the pasta. Using 2 forks, mix the pasta and sauce together gently but thoroughly. If the pasta seems too dry, add some of the reserved pasta cooking liquid by tablespoonfuls. Taste and adjust seasonings.

Divide the pasta among 4 heated plates and serve at once. Pass the cheese separately.

SWORDFISH

When my brother was very young, his ambition was to make his living catching swordfish. He outgrew that fantasy, but not his liking for this comparatively rare fish.

Atlantic swordfish, *xiphias gladius*, are a fisherman's dream. They are impressive jumpers and powerful fighters. Their sharp sword-like bills, often a third of the length of the fish, have been known to punch a hole in a boat.

Equipped with enormous eyes that enable them to pursue prey at great depths, swordfish roam most of the world's oceans and are usually found in offshore waters of southern Newfoundland during the summer months. They feed, primarily at night, on squid, herring, mackerel and many other fish.

Swordfish are very large. They can live to be more than twenty-five years old and weigh up to 1,200 pounds, although most commercially caught swordfish weigh much less than that. Female swordfish grow faster, live longer and are heavier than males.

The body of a swordfish is elongated and slightly compressed. The colour is variable, ranging from black to grey to a metallic purple or bronze. The body is dark above and pale below. The adult swordfish lacks both teeth and scales.

Swordfish is a culinary delight. Marketed both frozen and fresh, it is usually cut into steaks. The meat is firm and pinkish-tan in colour, with a unique flavor that is often compared to veal.

Swordfish is especially suited to grilling, but it may be pan-fried, poached or broiled. It gains extra flavour from marinades and sauces, but is good by itself with perhaps just a squeeze of lemon juice. Swordfish is best cut thick so that the meat does not dry out during cooking. It should never be overcooked. When ready to serve, the fish should still be quite moist.

GRILLED SWORDFISH WITH OLIVE RELISH
4 SERVINGS

- ½ cup drained bottled pimiento-stuffed green olives
- 1 large garlic clove, minced and mashed to a paste with a pinch of salt
- ¼ cup finely chopped fresh parsley
- ¼ cup extra-virgin olive oil
- 1 tablespoon freshly squeezed lemon juice
- Salt and freshly ground black pepper
- 4 6-ounce swordfish steaks (each about 1 inch thick)

The quickly grilled swordfish is lovely and moist and the piquant relish gives it an unusually bright burst of flavour.

In a food processor, pulse the olives until they are finely chopped. Add the garlic, parsley, 2 tablespoons of the olive oil and the lemon juice and pulse again until all the ingredients are well blended. Scrape the relish into a small bowl and set it aside at room temperature.

Prepare a hot grill.

Brush both sides of the swordfish steaks with the remaining oil and season them lightly with salt and pepper. Grill the fish on a rack set 5 to 6 inches over glowing coals for about 4 minutes on each side, or until just cooked through.

Serve the swordfish steaks topped with the relish.

Barbecued Swordfish Kebabs
4 Servings

Colourful kebabs are always popular barbecue fare. Serve these with a side dish of fluffy white rice.

- ¾ cup dry white wine
- 5 tablespoons extra-virgin olive oil
- ¼ cup lemon juice
- ¼ cup Worcestershire sauce
- 2 garlic cloves, minced
- ¼ teaspoon freshly ground black pepper
- 1½ pounds swordfish, cut into 1-inch cubes
- 1 large green bell pepper, cut into 1-inch pieces
- 16 cherry tomatoes
- 12 small button mushrooms
- Lemon wedges

In a large shallow bowl, whisk together the wine, olive oil, lemon juice, Worcestershire sauce, garlic and pepper. Add the fish, stirring to coat, and refrigerate, covered, for at least 1 hour and up to 6 hours.

Soak eight 9- or 10-inch bamboo skewers in water for 15 minutes.

Preheat a barbecue to moderate heat. Drain the fish, reserving the marinade. Thread the fish on the skewers, alternating the pieces of fish with the pieces of green pepper, the cherry tomatoes and the mushrooms.

Arrange the skewers on the grill. Grill, brushing frequently with the marinade, until the swordfish is just cooked through, about 7 minutes.

Serve the kebabs garnished with lemon wedges.

SWORDFISH STEAKS WITH CAPER SAUCE
4 SERVINGS

- 4 1-inch-thick swordfish steaks, each about 6 ounces
- Salt and freshly ground black pepper
- 2 tablespoons unsalted butter
- 1 tablespoon olive oil
- 6 shallots, thinly sliced
- ¾ cup dry white wine
- ¼ cup balsamic vinegar
- 2 tablespoons drained capers, chopped
- 2 tablespoons finely chopped fresh parsley

This takes only minutes to prepare, yet results in a main course with intense flavour. A simple side dish, such as rice or mashed potatoes, goes well here.

Pat the swordfish steaks dry and season them with salt and pepper.

In a large heavy frying pan, heat the butter and oil over moderate heat until the foam subsides and sauté the shallots, stirring, for 4 or 5 minutes, or until they are soft.

Push the shallots to one side of the frying pan. Add the swordfish steaks and sauté them for about 3 minutes. Using a wide spatula, turn the fish over gently and add the wine, vinegar and capers. Simmer the mixture for about 4 minutes longer, or until the fish is just cooked through.

Transfer the fish to heated plates. Stir the parsley into the sauce. Spoon the sauce over the fish and serve.

TUNA

The first tuna I knew came out of a can and was most often used as a sandwich filling or cooked in the dreaded "tuna casserole". Don't get me wrong, many wonderful recipes may be made with canned tuna and it is still very popular, but fresh tuna is becoming more available at markets and more people are discovering just how delicious it can be.

The bluefin tuna, *thunnus thynnus*, is found in small schools around Newfoundland and southern Labrador. Bluefin is prized as a sports fish and when one strikes, the battle can be spectacular. These giants are powerful enough to leap more than fifteen feet into the air. Bluefins are also taken commercially in traps, on longlines, or by purse-seine net.

This very beautiful, streamlined fish is one of the largest species of tuna, and one of the largest fish in the ocean, reaching lengths of up to ten feet and weights of close to 1,500 pounds. The upper part of the body is a shimmering blue while the underside is spotted and silvery. Tuna are extremely strong swimmers and many undertake considerable migrations. They feed, for the most part, on smaller schooling fish such as herring and mackerel.

Tuna meat varies both in colour and fat content, depending on the season and the diet. Tuna is at its fattest before spawning. Generally, the lighter it is in colour, the more delicate the taste and texture.

The meat of the bluefin tuna is almost beef-like, light to dark red in colour, with a firm texture and rich flavour.

When preparing fresh tuna, remove all residual blood by wiping the fish with a mixture of vinegar and water. It is also best to remove the dark midline strip of meat, which is oily and can taste bitter after cooking.

Fresh tuna may be grilled, poached or baked. It can also be eaten raw, in which case you should make certain that the tuna you are purchasing is "*sashimi* grade", that is, very fresh tuna of the choicest quality.

Canned tuna comes in several styles, either packed in oil or in water. "Solid" or "fancy" tuna means large pieces of meat, best for use in dishes specifying chunks of tuna. "Flaked" tuna is generally less expensive and is fine for sandwiches and salads.

TUNA PASTA SALAD

6 SERVINGS

This is one of the best pasta salads I know. Don't cut the recipe in half just because you have fewer than six people to serve. Tightly covered, the salad keeps well in the refrigerator for several days.

- ½ pound green beans, trimmed and cut diagonally into 1-inch pieces
- ¾ pound dried fusilli, or other corkscrew-shaped pasta
- 1 pound cooked tuna, or 2 7- ounce cans solid white tuna, drained
- 6 green onions, chopped, including about 1 inch of the green tops
- 1 large vine-ripened tomato, cored, seeded and diced
- ½ cup pitted black calamata olives, cut in halves
- ¾ cup mayonnaise, preferably homemade (see recipe index)
- 1 tablespoon balsamic vinegar
- 1 tablespoon freshly squeezed lemon juice
- ½ teaspoon celery salt
- Salt
- Freshly ground black pepper
- Lettuce leaves
- 1 tablespoon freshly grated parmesan cheese
- 1 tablespoon finely chopped parsley leaves

In a large pot of boiling salted water, cook the green beans until barely tender and still crisp, about 4 minutes. Using a slotted spoon, transfer the beans to a colander. Reserve the water in the pot. Drain the green beans and run them under cold water to cool them quickly and set their colour. Dry them on paper towels. Set the beans aside.

Bring the same pot of water to a boil. Add the pasta and cook it according to the package directions, until it is tender but still firm to the bite. Pour the pasta into same colander and rinse it under cold water to cool. Drain the pasta well.

Place the tuna in a large bowl and break it into small pieces. Add the green onions, tomato, black olives, pasta and green beans.

In a small bowl, mix together the mayonnaise, balsamic vinegar, lemon juice and celery salt. Pour the dressing over the salad and toss to combine. Add salt and freshly ground pepper to taste. Refrigerate the salad, covered, for at least 2 hours to allow the flavours to blend.

To serve, transfer the salad to an attractive shallow bowl lined with lettuce leaves. Mix the parmesan cheese and the parsley together and sprinkle the mixture on top of the salad.

Tuna Satés with Wasabi Sauce
4 Servings

- 1 cup mayonnaise, preferably homemade (see recipe index)
- 5 teaspoons soy sauce
- 1½ teaspoons sugar
- 2 teaspoons freshly squeezed lemon juice
- 1 tablespoon wasabi paste (Japanese green horseradish)
- A 1-pound tuna steak, cut into 1-inch cubes (about 24 cubes)
- 12 8- to 9-inch bamboo skewers, soaked in water 15 minutes

Wasabi, Japanese green horseradish, is an extremely hot, but rather addictive condiment. In oriental food shops, it can be found prepared in squeezable tubes or in powdered form to be mixed to a paste with water.

Rice is a natural accompaniment to this dish.

In a medium-sized bowl, stir together the mayonnaise, soy sauce, sugar, and lemon juice. Transfer ½ cup of the soy-mayonnaise mixture to a small bowl and stir in the *wasabi* paste. In a larger bowl, stir the tuna into the remaining soy-mayonnaise mixture. Refrigerate the *wasabi* sauce, covered, at least 1 hour and up to 1 day. Marinate the tuna, covered and refrigerated, for at least 1 hour and up to 4 hours.

Prepare a barbecue grill for moderately high heat.

Thread 2 tuna cubes onto each skewer, spacing them about 1 inch apart. Grill the tuna on an oiled rack set 5 to 6 inches over the coals until it is just cooked through, about 2 to 3 minutes per side.

Serve the tuna satés with the chilled *wasabi* sauce.

PAN-SEARED TUNA WITH BASIL OIL

4 SERVINGS

- 2 cups packed fresh basil leaves
- 1 cup extra-virgin olive oil
- 4 6-ounce sashimi-grade tuna steaks, cut 1 inch thick
- Salt
- Freshly ground black pepper
- 8 lemon wedges
- Wasabi paste (Japanese green horseradish), optional

Basil is one of our favourite herbs and my husband John and I usually grow several varieties and lots of it, starting the seeds indoors in early spring. We love the aroma and bright, clean flavour it lends to so many dishes. Any variety of basil, or a mixture of varieties, may be used in this recipe.

In a large saucepan, bring about 4 quarts of lightly salted water to a boil. While the is water heating, place 1 tray of ice cubes in a large bowl and fill the bowl ¾ full with cold water. When the water is boiling, add the basil leaves and cook them, stirring, only until they are wilted, about 1 minute. Drain the basil and immediately transfer it to the ice-water bath. Cool the basil in the ice water for 2 minutes. Drain the basil and squeeze out all the excess water. (This is easy to do by twisting it in the corner of a clean kitchen towel.)

In a blender or food processor, pulse the basil together with all but 1 tablespoon of the olive oil until well combined. Then strain the basil oil through a double thickness of cheesecloth or a coffee filter. Discard the solids and reserve the oil.

Heat a large heavy frying pan, preferably cast iron, over high heat until very hot. Season the tuna steaks on both sides with salt and pepper. Brush the steaks lightly all over with the reserved tablespoon of olive oil. Place the steaks in the hot pan and cook them until the bottom is brown and crusty, about 3 minutes. Turn the steaks and cook them for 1 minute longer. (The tuna will be just seared on the outside and raw in the centre.)

Transfer the tuna steaks to 4 heated plates. Drizzle each steak with some of the basil oil. Garnish each serving with 2 lemon wedges and, if desired, a small dab of *wasabi* paste.

TUNA AND POTATO STEW
4 SERVINGS

*Like most stews, this is as warming
as it is hearty.*

- 2 tablespoons olive oil
- 1 cup finely chopped onions
- 2 cloves garlic, minced
- 1 cup chopped, drained, canned tomatoes
- 3 medium-sized boiling potatoes, peeled and sliced into ¼-inch thick rounds
- ¼ teaspoon paprika
- 1 teaspoon salt
- Freshly ground black pepper
- 2 cups boiling water
- 1½ pounds fresh tuna, cut into 1-inch cubes
- 1 cup coarsely crumbled French-style bread
- 1 tablespoon finely chopped fresh parsley

In a heavy 3- to 4-quart saucepan, heat the olive oil over moderate heat. Add the onions and cook them, stirring, for about 5 minutes, or until they are soft but not brown. Stir in the garlic and cook 1 minute longer. Add the tomatoes, raise the heat and cook briskly, stirring, until most of the liquid in the pan has evaporated and the mixture is thick enough to hold its shape lightly in a spoon.

Add the potatoes and turn them about with a spoon until they are evenly coated with the tomato mixture. Stir in the paprika, salt and a generous grinding of black pepper. Pour in the boiling water. The liquid should just cover the potatoes; add a little more water if necessary.

Bring the mixture to a boil over high heat, cover the pan, reduce the heat to low and simmer the mixture for about 15 minutes, or until the potatoes are barely tender.

Stir the tuna into the stew. Cover the pan again and cook for 5 to 6 minutes longer, or until the tuna is cooked through. Taste for seasoning and add more salt if necessary.

To serve, ladle the stew into 4 heated shallow bowls. Top each serving with about ¼ cup of the bread crumbs and sprinkle with the parsley.

TUNA WITH TOMATO-HERB SAUCE

4 SERVINGS

Simple and quick to put together, this dish really wakes up the taste buds. Make sure the tomatoes are fully ripe and the best quality. And, above all, do not overcook the tuna.

- 3 tablespoons extra-virgin olive oil
- 1 large onion, thinly sliced
- 2 cloves garlic, minced
- ¼ cup finely chopped celery
- 3 large vine-ripened tomatoes, peeled, seeded and cut into ½-inch dice
- 1 bay leaf
- 1 cup chopped mixed fresh herbs, such as basil, tarragon, mint and parsley
- Salt
- Freshly ground black pepper.
- 4 6-ounce pieces tuna steak, cut about 1 inch thick
- Fresh basil or tarragon sprigs for garnish

In a large heavy frying pan, heat 2 tablespoons of the olive oil over moderate heat. Add the onion, garlic and celery. Sauté the vegetables until they are tender but not brown, about 10 minutes. Add the tomatoes and the bay leaf. Partially cover the pan and cook over low heat, stirring occasionally, until the mixture has thickened, about 15 minutes. Remove and discard the bay leaf. Stir in the herbs. Season the sauce to taste with salt and pepper. Keep the sauce warm over low heat.

Sprinkle the tuna with salt and pepper. In another large heavy frying pan, heat the remaining tablespoon of olive oil over moderately high heat. Add the tuna steaks and cook them until lightly browned and just opaque in the centre, about 3 minutes per side.

Transfer the tuna to a heated platter or heated individual plates. Spoon the sauce over the tuna and garnish with the herb sprigs.

WOLF FISH

It is often said that only a wolf fish could love another wolf fish. Named for their vicious-looking heads and canine-like teeth, they're certainly not attractive creatures. In fact, the wolf fish is rather frightening to look at, with its squat, misshapen body and large bulbous head. But if you've never tasted this fish, it's definitely worth buying for its deliciously sweet and tender meat.

Atlantic wolf fish, *anarhichas lupus,* goes by a number of other names, among them Atlantic catfish, ocean catfish, Atlantic lobo or Atlantic *loup de mer* (not to be confused with the French *loup de mer,* which is actually a sea bass).

Found in waters all around Newfoundland and southern Labrador, Atlantic wolf fish are nonmigratory and live on the bottom of the ocean in depths of up to 350 feet. Harvested as part of the traditional bottom trawl fishery, their average commercial weight is between four and eight pounds, providing rather large fillets.

Wolf fish are somewhat dull-coloured, ranging from grey to brown, with dark vertical bands along their sides. The skin is tough and leathery. They feed mostly on molluscs and crustaceans. They tend to be solitary in nature and are not as abundant as other groundfish species, such as cod and haddock.

Atlantic wolf fish fillets are firm and the bones can be easily felt and removed. The meat is very white, lean and somewhat sweet. When cooked, the fish flakes like cod, but the flakes are smaller.

Wolf fish can be used with success in almost any recipe that specifies white firm-fleshed fish. It may be grilled, baked, poached or sautéed and adapts well to many sauces, particularly those with tomatoes and herbs.

WOLF FISH AND LEEK SOUP

6 SERVINGS

Country bread and a cheese platter make this an easy, but delicious luncheon or supper.

- 3 tablespoons unsalted butter
- 3 medium-sized leeks, white and pale green parts only, thinly sliced
- 1 pound boiling potatoes, peeled and cut into ½-inch dice
- 4 cups basic fish stock (see recipe index), or bottled clam juice diluted with water
- 2 tablespoons chopped fresh thyme leaves, or 2 teaspoons dried thyme
- 1 cup heavy cream
- 1 pound wolf fish fillets, cut into 1-inch pieces
- Salt
- Freshly ground black pepper
- Snipped fresh chives

In a large heavy saucepan, melt the butter over moderate heat. Add the leeks and stir to coat them with the butter. Cover the leeks and cook them over low heat until they begin to soften, about 5 minutes. Add the diced potatoes, fish stock or clam juice and thyme. Bring the mixture to a boil over high heat. Partially cover the saucepan, reduce the heat to low and simmer for 5 minutes. Add the cream and return the soup to a simmer. Add the wolf fish and simmer uncovered until the potatoes are tender and the fish is cooked through, about 5 or 6 minutes longer.

Taste the soup for seasoning and add salt, if necessary, and a generous grinding of black pepper. Ladle the soup into heated bowls. Garnish each serving with a few snipped chives.

WOLF FISH WITH TOMATO-ZUCCHINI SAUCE
6 SERVINGS

- 3 tablespoons olive oil
- 1 medium-sized onion, coarsely chopped
- 4 cloves garlic, minced
- 3 small zucchini, trimmed but unpeeled, cut into ½-inch dice
- 1 tablespoon chopped fresh basil leaves
- 1 28-ounce can diced tomatoes, drained, with ½ cup juice reserved
- 2 pounds wolf fish fillets, cut into serving-sized pieces
- Salt
- Freshly ground black pepper
- Whole fresh basil leaves for garnish

This Mediterranean-flavoured entrée is a great summer dish. It's especially useful to keep in mind when your garden is overflowing with ripe zucchini, a most prolific vegetable.

In a large heavy frying pan, heat the oil over moderate heat. Add the onion and garlic and cook, stirring occasionally, until the onion is soft but not brown, about 5 minutes. Add the zucchini and chopped basil leaves and cook, stirring occasionally, until the zucchini begins to soften, about 5 minutes. Add the tomatoes and the reserved juice and bring the mixture to a boil.

Season the fish on both sides with salt and pepper. Place the fish pieces on top of the vegetables in the frying pan. Cover the frying pan, reduce the heat to low and simmer until the fish is just cooked through, 6 to 10 minutes, depending on the thickness of the fillets. Transfer the fish pieces to a platter and keep them warm in a low oven.

Bring the mixture remaining in the frying pan to a boil over moderately high heat. Continue to boil, stirring, until the mixture has thickened to sauce consistency, about 5 minutes.

Taste for seasoning and spoon the sauce over the fish. Garnish the platter with whole fresh basil leaves.

SPICE-CRUMBED WOLF FISH

6 SERVINGS

- 2 pounds wolf fish fillets, about 1 inch thick
- 3 eggs
- 1 cup coarse saltine cracker crumbs
- 1½ tablespoons chili powder
- 2 teaspoons ground cumin
- ½ teaspoon freshly ground black pepper
- ¼ cup vegetable oil, plus more if necessary
- Lemon wedges
- Fresh cilantro sprigs

A highly seasoned coating seals in the flavour and keeps the fish very moist. To make the crumbs, place the crackers in a heavy plastic bag or between pieces of waxed paper and crush them with a rolling pin.

Cut the fish fillets into serving-sized pieces and dry the pieces well on paper towels.

In a large shallow bowl, beat the eggs with a fork until they are just blended. Place the cracker crumbs in a separate large shallow bowl. In a small bowl, stir together the chili powder, cumin and black pepper. Sprinkle the fish pieces generously with the spice mixture, rubbing it in with your fingers. Dip the fish pieces into the eggs, then into the cracker crumbs to coat completely. Transfer the fish pieces to waxed paper.

In a large heavy frying pan over moderately high heat, heat the ¼ cup of vegetable oil. Working in batches, fry the fish pieces in a single layer, turning them once and regulating the heat so they do not scorch, until the pieces are golden brown and just opaque in the centre, about 5 minutes per side. Add more oil to the pan between batches if necessary. Transfer the cooked fish to a platter lined with paper towel. Keep it warm in a low oven until all the fish is fried.

When ready to serve, garnish the wolf fish with lemon wedges and cilantro sprigs.

MIXED SEAFOOD

There is always something luxurious about a mixed seafood dish, perhaps because it usually includes expensive items like lobster or scallops. But many famous mixed seafood dishes—French *bouillabaisse* and Spanish *paella*, for example—originated as simple fishermen's meals, made from by-catch or from the seafood left over at the end of the day when the rest of the catch had been sold.

Although all of these recipes specify several varieties of seafood, they are flexible enough that you can make substitutions with fish and shellfish of similar taste and texture. If you can't find clams in your market, for example, buy some extra mussels. If cod is not available, you might substitute haddock or hake. Lobster could be replaced by large shrimp.

So long as you use your instincts and season carefully, you will create the harmony of flavours essential to any good mixed seafood dish.

CHILLED SEAFOOD SOUP WITH VEGETABLES

4 SERVINGS

- 1 large ear fresh corn
- 2 pounds vine-ripened tomatoes, cored and coarsely chopped
- 1 small red onion, coarsely chopped
- 1 large cucumber, seeded and coarsely chopped
- 1 large green pepper, seeded and coarsely chopped
- 2 cloves garlic, coarsely chopped
- ½ cup loosely packed fresh parsley leaves
- 1 tablespoon extra-virgin olive oil
- 3½ cups tomato juice
- Salt
- Freshly ground black pepper
- Tabasco sauce to taste (optional)
- 1½ cups cooked shellfish (crabmeat, shrimp or lobster, or a combination)
- ¼ cup packed fresh basil leaves, shredded

This refreshing soup was created with summer and lunch on the patio in mind. It relies on fresh vegetables, the fresher the better, and requires no cooking, an extra advantage to dining on hot and humid days.

Any leftover shellfish, preferably a combination of varieties, is delicious in this recipe.

Using a sharp knife, cut the kernels from the corn ear. Set the corn kernels aside in a small bowl.

In a food processor, pulse together about half of the tomatoes, the onion, cucumber and green pepper until finely chopped, but not puréed. (The vegetables should retain some texture and crunch.) Transfer the mixture to a large bowl. Without rinsing the food processor, pulse the remaining tomatoes with the garlic, parsley and olive oil until smoothly blended. Add the mixture to the bowl and stir to combine with the other ingredients. Stir in the tomato juice.

Season the soup to taste with salt and pepper and Tabasco sauce, if desired. (You may prefer to pass the Tabasco sauce separately at the table.) Chill the soup for at least 4 hours or until it is very cold.

When ready to serve the soup, stir in the shellfish. Ladle the soup into 4 chilled soup bowls and sprinkle each serving with some of the corn kernels. Garnish each serving with shredded basil leaves.

Seafood Chowder with Screech
8 to 10 Servings

Unusually long cooking is the secret to this truly marvellous chowder.

- 2 pounds mussels, preferably cultivated, in their shells
- 3 tablespoons unsalted butter
- 1 medium-sized onion, coarsely chopped
- 1 green bell pepper, coarsely chopped
- 1 large leek, white and pale green parts only, thinly sliced
- 2 medium-sized carrots, coarsely chopped
- 1 celery stalk, coarsely chopped
- 1 medium tomato, peeled, seeded and diced
- 3 large garlic cloves, minced
- 6 cups basic fish stock (see recipe index)
- 2 pounds cod fillets, skin and bones removed
- 5 tablespoons tomato paste
- 1 bay leaf, 15 whole allspice and 1 teaspoon dried thyme, tied in cheesecloth
- 3 tablespoons cornstarch stirred together with 3 tablespoons water
- 1 pound small to medium shrimp, shelled and deveined
- 3 tablespoons Worcestershire sauce
- ¼ cup dark rum, preferably Newfoundland Screech
- 1 teaspoon hot pepper sauce, or to taste

Scrub the mussels under cold water and pull off the beards. In a large heavy pot, combine the mussels with 2 cups of water and bring them to a boil over high heat. Cover the pot and steam just until they open, 3 to 4 minutes. Drain the mussels in a large sieve set over a bowl to catch all the liquid. When the mussels are cool enough to handle, remove and discard the shells. Set the mussels and reserved cooking liquid aside in separate containers.

Rinse out the pot and melt the butter in it over moderately low heat. Add the onion, pepper, leek, carrots, celery, chopped tomato and garlic. Cook the vegetables, covered, until softened, about 7 or 8 minutes. Stir in the fish stock and the reserved mussel liquid. Raise the heat to moderate and bring the mixture to a simmer. Simmer, uncovered, 20 minutes.

Stir in the cod, tomato paste and cheesecloth bag of spices. Simmer 20 minutes (the fish will break up). Stir the cornstarch mixture and add it to the chowder. Simmer, stirring, for about 2 minutes. Stir in the reserved mussels, shrimp, Worcestershire sauce and rum and gently simmer 30 minutes longer. Remove the chowder from the heat and let it stand, covered, for at least 1 hour to blend the flavours. Gently return it to a simmer. Taste for seasoning, adding salt if necessary, and stir in the hot pepper sauce to taste.

Serve the chowder from a large heated soup tureen.

NEWFOUNDLAND BOUILLABAISSE
6 TO 8 SERVINGS

Although bouillabaisse is a Mediterranean specialty, this recipe gives some North Atlantic substitutions for the typical fish.

- 3 pounds of non-oily assorted fish fillets, such cod, haddock or flounder
- ¾ pound shrimp, shelled and deveined
- ½ cup extra-virgin olive oil
- 1½ cups dry white wine
- 3 fresh thyme sprigs, chopped, or substitute ½ teaspoon dried thyme
- 3 garlic cloves, minced
- 1 teaspoon fennel seeds
- 1 tablespoon coarsely chopped orange peel, without any white pith
- ¼ teaspoon saffron threads
- 2 tablespoons unsalted butter
- 3 medium-sized leeks, white and pale green parts only, thinly sliced
- 1½ cups drained canned tomatoes
- 4 cups boiling fish stock, or shellfish stock (see recipe index)
- 2 dozen mussels, in their shells, debearded and scrubbed
- 1 dozen clams in their shells, scrubbed
- 6 to 8 ½-inch-thick slices French-style bread, toasted until crisp
- Rouille (see recipe index)

Cut the fish fillets into large pieces. Lay the fish pieces and the shrimp in a large shallow bowl. In a non-reactive bowl, whisk together the next 7 ingredients. Pour the mixture over the fish, turning it around with a large spoon to coat completely. Cover the seafood and refrigerate for 1 hour.

In a large heavy pot, melt the butter over moderate heat. Add the leeks and cook them, stirring, until they are soft but not brown. Stir in the tomatoes and cook until most of the liquid has evaporated. Add the marinated seafood along with the marinade ingredients. Pour on the boiling stock. Bring the mixture to a boil and boil it rapidly for 10 minutes. Add the mussels and clams, partially cover, reduce the

heat and simmer gently for 5 or 6 minutes, or until the shellfish open. Using a slotted spoon, remove the fish and shellfish to a heated platter. Cover the platter and keep it warm in a low oven.

Strain the broth remaining in the pot into a large saucepan, pressing down hard on the ingredients before discarding them. Bring the broth to a simmer, taste and adjust seasonings and pour it into a heated soup tureen.

To serve the *bouillabaisse*, place a slice of toasted bread in each heated soup bowl. Arrange a serving of fish and shellfish from the platter on top. Then ladle on some broth. A spoonful of *rouille* may be spread on the toast before adding the seafood or it may be passed separately.

MIXED SEAFOOD SALAD

6 TO 8 SERVINGS

- 1 pound cleaned squid, fresh or frozen, thawed, cut into ¼-inch rings
- 1 pound medium-sized shrimp
- 1 pound mussels, scrubbed and debearded
- 1 pound very fresh whole bay scallops, or sea scallops, sliced
- 1 cup freshly squeezed lime juice (juice of about 6 limes)
- 1 medium-sized green pepper, finely chopped
- 1 medium-sized red pepper, finely chopped
- ¼ cup finely chopped shallots or red onion
- ¼ cup finely chopped parsley leaves
- 6 tablespoons extra-virgin olive oil
- 1 tablespoon red wine vinegar
- 1 teaspoon salt
- ½ teaspoon dried summer savory
- Freshly ground black pepper
- Small head romaine lettuce

In this fabulous salad, the scallops are "cooked" only in ceviche, that is, marinated in citrus juice, so it is essential that they be very fresh.

In a large saucepan, cook the squid and shrimp in salted boiling water for 2 minutes. Drain them well and reserve the cooking liquid. Peel the shrimp and remove the intestinal tract from the outer side. Set the shrimp and squid aside.

Pour the reserved cooking liquid back into the saucepan. Add the mussels, cover the pot, and cook them just until they are all open, about 4 to 5 minutes. Remove the mussels and drain them. Remove and discard their shells. Discard the cooking liquid.

In a large non-reactive bowl, combine the scallops, squid, shrimp and mussels. Pour in the lime juice and toss gently to combine. Cover the bowl with plastic wrap and refrigerate the mixture for at least 2 hours to blend the flavours.

Meanwhile, in a bowl, combine the green and red pepper, the shallots or onion and the parsley. Stir in the oil, vinegar, salt, savory and black pepper to taste. Add this mixture to the marinated salad and toss lightly. Cover and refrigerate again for at least 1 hour.

About a half hour before serving, remove the salad from the refrigerator to take the chill off. Taste and adjust seasonings. Serve the salad on lettuce-lined plates.

SEAFOOD ELEGANTÉ

8 TO 10 SERVINGS

- 1 pound frozen bay scallops, thawed only until they can be separated
- ½ cup plus 2 tablespoons unsalted butter
- 2 10-ounce cans whole button mushrooms, drained well
- ¾ cup all-purpose flour
- 2 teaspoons salt
- 4 cups milk, heated to a simmer
- 3 tablespoons tomato paste
- 1 tablespoon lemon juice, or substitute ¼ cup dry white wine
- 2 teaspoons Worcestershire sauce
- 2 5-ounce cans lobster, drained
- 2 5-ounce cans shrimp, drained

The beauty of this recipe is that it can be made completely from items you've stocked in the cupboard and freezer. It's especially handy to have in your culinary repertoire for an occasion when a hungry crowd shows up unexpectedly. And, although many of the ingredients come out of a can, the taste is totally homemade.

The recipe is from my mother-in-law, Cec King, a wonderful cook. She suggests serving it over rice or noodles.

In a medium-sized saucepan, cook the partially thawed scallops in lightly salted simmering water for 3 or 4 minutes, or just until they turn opaque and are barely cooked through. Drain the scallops and set them aside.

In a frying pan, sauté the mushrooms in 2 tablespoons of the butter until they are golden. Set the mushrooms aside.

In a large pot, melt the remaining ½ cup of butter over moderate heat. When the foam begins to subside, add the flour and salt and, stirring constantly with a wire whisk, cook the mixture for about 2 minutes. Do not let it brown. Remove the mixture from the heat and pour in the heated milk all at once, whisking vigorously to incorporate it. Return the saucepan to high heat and continue whisking until the sauce comes to a boil and is thick and smooth. Reduce the heat to low and add the tomato paste, Worcestershire sauce and lemon juice, or wine, whisking to combine the ingredients well. Fold in the scallops, sautéed mushrooms, lobster and shrimp and cook gently just until the ingredients are heated through. Taste and adjust the seasonings. Serve at once over rice or noodles.

SEAFOOD CRÊPES
4 SERVINGS

This is a heavenly recipe and one of my all-time favourites.

- 4 tablespoons unsalted butter
- ¼ cup finely chopped shallots or red onion
- 1 clove garlic, minced
- 1 small salmon fillet, about 4 ounces, cut into ½-inch pieces
- 1 small cod or haddock fillet, about 4 ounces, cut into ½-inch pieces
- ¾ pound small to medium shrimp, peeled and deveined

- ½ pound bay scallops
- 1 cup dry white wine
- ¾ cup heavy cream
- 2 egg yolks
- Salt and freshly ground black pepper
- Drops freshly squeezed lemon juice to taste
- 8 9-inch cooked thin crêpes
- ½ cup grated gruyère cheese

In a large non-reactive saucepan, heat 3 tablespoons of the butter over moderately low heat. Add the shallots or onion and garlic and cook them for about 5 minutes, or until they begin to soften. Add the salmon and cod pieces and cook, stirring, until they are just opaque. Pour in the wine and let it sizzle briefly. Add the shrimp and scallops. Reduce the heat and simmer the mixture very gently for 2 to 3 minutes, or until the seafood is just cooked through. Using a slotted spoon, remove the seafood to a bowl and set it aside.

Over high heat, boil the liquid in the saucepan until reduced by half. Reduce the heat to low and add ½ cup of the cream, stirring to heat through. Stir ½ cup of the mixture into the seafood. Keep the remaining sauce warm.

In a small bowl, mix the egg yolks with the remaining ¼ cup of cream. Stir 2 tablespoons of the warm sauce into the egg-yolk mixture.

Then pour the egg-yolk mixture back into the remaining sauce. Bring the sauce to a boil over moderate heat, whisking constantly, until it will coat a spoon thickly. Season the sauce to taste with salt, pepper and drops of lemon juice. Set the seafood mixture and the sauce aside.

Preheat the oven to 375°F. Grease a large rectangular or oval baking dish with the remaining tablespoon of butter. Place a portion of the seafood mixture along the centre of each *crêpe*, dividing it equally. Roll the *crêpes* around the seafood. Place the filled *crêpes* side by side, seam side down, in the baking dish. Cover them with the sauce and sprinkle on the cheese. Bake the *crêpes* for about 25 minutes, or until the cheese is bubbling.

Serve the *crêpes* at once directly from the baking dish.

DEEP-FRIED MIXED SEAFOOD
ABOUT 4 SERVINGS

- 1 cup sifted all-purpose flour
- ¾ cup lukewarm water
- 3 tablespoons olive oil
- ½ teaspoon salt
- 1 egg white
- 1 pound squid, bodies cut into 1/2-inch rings and tentacles left whole
- ½ pound cod or haddock fillets, cut into 11/2-inch strips
- ½ pound medium-sized shrimp, shelled and deveined
- ½ pound small smelts, cleaned and left whole, but with heads removed
- Vegetable oil for deep-frying
- Lemon wedges

I was introduced to this tasty treat in Italy, where it's called "fritto misto di pesce" and is often sold from vehicles similar to our "chip wagons". Italians use a variety of small whole fish and octopus in fritto misto. I've substituted seafood found in Newfoundland waters.

In a large bowl, stir together the flour, warm water, olive oil and salt just until the mixture is smooth and creamy. Do not overstir. Set the batter aside to rest at room temperature for about 1 hour.

In a large saucepan, bring 1 quart of water to a boil. Drop in the squid, partially cover the pot and let the squid simmer gently for 30 minutes. (They should be quite tender.) Drain the squid pieces well and dry them between pieces of paper towel. Set the squid aside. Dry the cod or haddock, the shrimp and the smelts and set them aside separately.

Using an electric beater or balloon whisk, beat the egg white until it is very stiff and fold it into the batter.

In a deep fryer or a large pot, heat 3 inches of vegetable oil to 375ºF on a deep-frying thermometer. Preheat the oven to 250°F and line a large baking sheet with paper towels. Deep-fry the squid, cod or haddock, shrimp and smelt separately, first dropping 5 or 6 pieces into the batter and turning them about with a spoon. When they are coated, lift them out and let the excess batter drain off before placing them in the hot oil. Deep-fry the seafood, turning the pieces occasionally, for about 5 minutes, or until they are golden brown. With tongs, transfer the fried pieces to the towel-lined baking sheet and keep them warm in the oven while you fry the remainder. Let the oil return to 375°F before adding more seafood.

When all the seafood is fried, serve it from a napkin-lined platter and garnish with lemon wedges.

Portuguese Fish Stew with Sausage
4 Servings

- ¼ cup dry white wine
- ¼ teaspoon saffron threads, crushed
- 3 tablespoons olive oil
- 1 large onion, coarsely chopped
- 3 cloves garlic, minced
- 3 cups basic fish stock (see recipe index)
- 1 14-ounce can diced tomatoes in juice
- ½ pound linguiça or chorizo sausage, cut into ¼-inch-thick slices
- 2 dozen mussels, preferably cultivated, scrubbed and debearded
- 1 dozen clams, scrubbed
- ½ cup cornmeal
- Salt and freshly ground black pepper
- ½ pound cod fillets, cut into pieces about 3 inches square
- 2 tablespoons chopped fresh parsley

The Portuguese fished in Newfoundland waters for centuries. Although they never settled here in any numbers, they did leave a certain legacy.

In a small saucepan, bring the wine to a simmer. Stir in the saffron. Remove the saucepan from the heat, cover it and let it stand for 15 minutes.

Heat 1 tablespoon of the olive oil in a large heavy saucepan over moderate heat. Add the chopped onion and garlic cook, stirring, for about 5 minutes, or they are soft but not brown. Add the fish stock, the tomatoes and their juices, and the saffron-wine mixture. Simmer the ingredients over moderately low heat, uncovered, for 20 minutes. Add the sausage, mussels and clams. Cover the pot, raise the heat to high and cook until the shellfish open, about 6 minutes. Discard any that do not open.

Meanwhile, spread the cornmeal on a piece of waxed paper or a plate. Season it with salt and freshly ground pepper. Dip each side of the fish fillet pieces in the cornmeal to coat them lightly, shaking off the excess.

In a large heavy frying pan, heat the remaining 2 tablespoons of oil over moderately high heat. Add the fish pieces and cook them until golden brown, about 3 minutes per side. Ladle 1 cup of broth from the saucepan over the fish, cover the pan and cook for 5 minutes longer.

Transfer the fish pieces to 4 heated shallow bowls. Arrange the clams, mussels and sausage around the fish. Top with the remaining broth and sprinkle each serving with a little chopped parsley.

PAELLA
4 TO 6 SERVINGS

A one-pan meal, paella may be as simple or elaborate as you wish. Lobster may be added, or rabbit could replace the chicken.

- 6 tablespoons olive oil
- ½ pound garlic-seasoned smoked pork sausage, preferably chorizo, cut into 1/4-inch slices
- 3 chicken legs, thighs and drumsticks separated
- 1 medium-sized onion, finely chopped
- 2 cloves garlic, finely chopped
- 1 small yellow pepper, cut into small dice
- 1 large tomato, peeled, seeded and chopped
- 2 cups medium- to long-grain white rice
- ¼ teaspoon saffron threads, pulverized, dissolved in 4 cups hot fish stock
- 12 large shrimp, in their shells
- 12 clams, in their shells, purged of sand, scrubbed
- 24 mussels, preferably cultivated, in their shells, scrubbed and debearded
- 1 large green pepper, cut lengthwise into ½-inch strips.
- Lemon wedges for garnish

Preheat the oven to 400°F.

In a heavy *paella* pan, about 14-inches in diameter, or a shallow roasting pan, heat 4 tablespoons of the olive oil over moderately high heat. Fry the sausage slices, turning them, until they are well browned on both sides. With a slotted spoon, remove the sausage and set it aside to drain on paper towels. Add the chicken pieces to the fat remaining in the pan and brown them well on all sides. Remove the chicken to a plate and set it aside.

Add the onion, garlic, yellow pepper and tomato to the pan, stirring over moderate heat for 3 or 4 minutes, or until the vegetables begin to soften. Raise the heat and cook, stirring, until most of the liquid has evaporated. With a slotted spoon, remove the vegetable mixture to a dish and set it aside.

Add the remaining 2 tablespoons of olive oil to the pan. Stir in the rice and stir gently, over low heat, until the rice is thoroughly coated with the oil. Stir in the vegetable mixture and the hot saffron-fish stock. Remove the pan from the heat. Arrange the sausage, chicken pieces and shrimp on top of the rice. Push the clams and mussels down into the rice, interspersed them evenly among the other ingredients. Scatter the strips of green pepper on top.

Bake the *paella*, uncovered, on the lowest shelf of the oven, for 35 minutes, or until the rice is just tender. Remove the pan from the oven and drape a clean kitchen towel over it. Let the *paella* rest for 10 minutes.

Garnish the *paella* with lemon wedges and serve it from the pan.

Linguine with Mixed Seafood Sauce
6 Servings

*Designed as a main course, this will
serve ten people as a first course.*

- ¼ cup extra-virgin olive oil
- 3 garlic cloves, minced
- 1 pound cleaned squid, bodies cut into ½-inch-wide rings, tentacles chopped
- 1¼ cups dry white wine
- 1 28-ounce can plum tomatoes
- 1 teaspoon dried basil
- ½ teaspoon dried crushed red pepper
- 1 tablespoon tomato paste
- 1¼ cup water
- 1½ pounds mussels, scrubbed and debearded

- 1 uncooked lobster tail, shelled and meat cut into 1-inch pieces
- ½ pound uncooked large shrimp, peeled and deveined
- ½ pound whole bay scallops, or sea scallops cut into quarters
- ¼ cup chopped fresh parsley, preferably flat-leafed Italian parsley
- Salt and freshly ground black pepper
- 1 pound dried linguine

Heat 3 tablespoons of the oil in large frying pan over moderate heat. Add the garlic and stir just until it begins to soften. Add the squid and cook just until they become opaque, about 3 minutes. Add the wine, reduce the heat to low and simmer, uncovered, until the liquid is reduced by half, about 20 minutes. Add the tomatoes with their juice, the basil, crushed red pepper and tomato paste. Bring the mixture to a simmer again, breaking up the tomatoes with a spoon. Cover the pan and simmer over low heat for 40 minutes longer.

Bring ¼ cup water to boil in a large non-reactive pot over high heat. Add the mussels. Cover the pot and cook until the mussels open, about 5 minutes. (Discard any mussels that do not open.) Transfer the mussels to a colander set over a bowl and let them drain.

Reserve the mussel liquid.

When the squid and tomato mixture has cooked, strain the reserved mussel liquid through a fine sieve into the tomato mixture. Simmer the mixture, uncovered, until slightly thickened, about 10 minutes. Add the lobster, shrimp and scallops. Simmer 2 minutes. Do not overcook. Add the mussels and simmer 1 minute longer. Stir in the remaining oil and the parsley. Season the sauce to taste with salt and pepper.

Meanwhile, cook the linguine in a large pot of boiling salted water until just tender but still firm to the bite. Drain the linguine and return it to the pot. Add the sauce and toss gently to coat. Serve on heated pasta plates.

Seafood Risotto
4 to 6 Servings

The best risotto I've ever eaten was made with seafood in a small Italian restaurant. This is my version. To retain its characteristic creaminess, risotto must be served as soon as it is done.

- 2 cups basic shellfish stock (see recipe index)
- ¾ teaspoon salt
- 3 cups water
- 3 tablespoons olive oil
- 2 tablespoons unsalted butter
- 1 cup finely chopped leeks, white and pale green parts only
- 1½ cups arborio rice (Italian short-grain rice)
- ½ cup dry white wine
- 1 14-ounce can diced tomatoes
- 3 cloves garlic, minced
- ¾ pound small shrimp, peeled and deveined
- ¾ pound sea scallops, cut into quarters, or whole bay scallops
- 3 tablespoons finely chopped parsley, preferably Italian flat-leaf parsley

In a medium-sized non-reactive saucepan, combine the stock, salt and water and bring to a simmer. Keep the broth hot over low heat.

In a large heavy saucepan, heat 1 tablespoon of the olive oil and the butter together over moderate heat. Add the leeks and sauté them until they are soft, about 4 minutes. Add the rice and sauté, stirring, for about 2 minutes, or until the grains are coated in oil and butter. Add the wine, stirring until it is absorbed. Add the tomatoes and cook, stirring, until their liquid is absorbed.

Add 1 cup of the hot broth to the rice. Simmer until the liquid is absorbed, stirring often. Continue adding the broth by ½ cupfuls until you have used all but ½ cup. Simmer until most of the liquid is absorbed before each addition and stir often. Cook until the rice is almost tender, but still slightly firm to the bite. (This will take about 18 minutes.)

Meanwhile, heat the remaining 2 tablespoons of oil in a frying pan over moderate heat. Add the garlic and sauté it until it begins to soften. Add the shrimp and scallops and sauté them, stirring, for 4 about minutes. (The seafood will not be fully cooked, but will continue to cook in the *risotto*.) Mix the seafood into the rice. Cook for about 3 minutes longer. The mixture should be very creamy. If it is not, stir in a little more of the broth.

Remove the *risotto* from the heat. Stir in the chopped parsley. Taste and adjust the seasonings. Transfer the *risotto* to a heated serving bowl and serve it immediately, while it is still creamy.

STOCKS & SAUCES

The wonderful flavour of a good seafood dish is often the result of the stock used for its cooking or the sauce that enhances it.

A stock is the liquid obtained from simmering together fish trimmings and/or seafood shells with vegetables, seasonings and water. The liquid is strained and boiled down, if necessary, to concentrate its flavour. Stocks may be used to moisten seafood while cooking or used as a base for stews, chowders or sauces.

Stocks are easy to make and can simmer away with very little attention. The trick is slow cooking, which pries the protein and gelatin from the bones or shells, coaxing out the essence. It's usually worth the effort to make a large pot of stock and freeze some for future use.

The shells of almost all shellfish greatly enhance any stock. If I have lobster, crab or shrimp shells, for example, left over from some other recipe I'm preparing, I wrap them air-tightly and freeze them until I have enough to add to fresh fish trimmings for a good rich stock. The shells should not be kept frozen for more than a month or so, however.

The role of a sauce is to complement the taste of the seafood, to contrast with it or to give variety to its presentation. Sauces can add freshness or a touch of whimsy and make a more interesting dish out of simply prepared food.

Rich sauces should be used sparingly so as not to overpower the delicate flavour and texture of most fish and shellfish. A sauce should never be used as a mask or to disguise the taste of any food.

The stocks and sauces presented here are by no means exhaustive, but they do represent some favourites from my own repertoire.

BASIC FISH STOCK
ABOUT 6 CUPS

- 2 tablespoons olive oil
- 2½ to 3 pounds bones and trimmings from any white-fleshed fish, such as cod or flounder, chopped into pieces
- 1½ cups sliced onions
- 1 carrot, coarsely chopped
- 1 stalk celery, coarsely chopped
- About 15 parsley sprigs with long stems
- ½ teaspoon fennel seeds
- ½ teaspoon salt
- 3 tablespoons freshly squeezed lemon juice
- 8 cups water

Fish stock is essential to a number of recipes in this book. Powdered seafood stock, found in many large supermarkets, may be substituted, but the flavour will be better and fresher if you make your own.

This basic stock contains only a small amount of salt because many preparations require it to be reduced, which could make it too salty. The stock will keep for several days in the refrigerator, tightly covered, and may be frozen for up to three months.

Pour the oil into a heavy-bottomed 4- to 5-quart non-reactive pot. Tilt the pot to coat the sides about half way up with the oil. Add the fish bones and trimmings, onions, carrot, celery, parsley, fennel seeds, salt and lemon juice. Stir to mix. Over moderate heat, cook the mixture, covered, for 5 minutes. Add the water. Bring the mixture to a boil, skimming off and discarding the foam and scum. Boil rapidly for 5 minutes. Reduce the heat to moderately low and, skimming occasionally, simmer the stock, uncovered, for 20 minutes longer.

Pour the stock through a sieve lined with a double thickness of damp cheesecloth into a large bowl, pressing down hard on the solids with the back of a spoon to extract all their flavour. Discard the solids. Let the stock cool to room temperature, uncovered, before ladling it into appropriate-sized containers to refrigerate or freeze.

COURT BOUILLON
ABOUT 6 CUPS

- 1 large carrot, peeled and coarsely chopped
- 1 medium-sized onion, peeled and coarsely chopped
- 1 stalk celery, coarsely chopped
- 1 bay leaf
- ½ teaspoon fennel seeds
- 10 black peppercorns
- 2 teaspoons salt
- 5 cups water
- 2 cups white wine

Court bouillon is literally "quick broth", not really a stock because it contains no seafood, but water enhanced with wine and seasonings. It is used for poaching seafood, especially whole fish.

Court bouillon may be made a day ahead of the time you wish to use it. Allow it to cool to room temperature and then refrigerate it in a covered container. It should always be brought to a simmer before the fish is immersed in it. If the fish is large, adjust the quantities so there is enough liquid to completely cover the fish.

In a large non-reactive saucepan, combine all the ingredients. Bring the mixture to a rapid boil. Partially cover the pot, reduce the heat to a slow simmer and simmer for 20 minutes.

Using a colander lined with a double thickness of cheesecloth, strain the broth into a large bowl or into the pan in which you intend to poach the seafood. Press down hard on the solids to extract all their flavour. Discard the solids.

Taste the *court bouillon* and adjust the seasonings. It should be rather salty.

SHELLFISH STOCK
ABOUT 4 CUPS

This rich stock can be made easily from shells you've frozen, tightly wrapped, until you have enough. Once the stock is made, it too may be frozen, for up to three months.

- 2 tablespoons cooking oil
- The chopped or smashed leftover shells and bodies from 1 or 2 cooked lobsters, or the shells from 1 pound shrimp, or a combination of both
- 1 medium-sized leek, white and pale green parts only, coarsely chopped
- 1 small onion, coarsely chopped
- 1 clove garlic, chopped
- 1 celery stalk, coarsely chopped
- 1 medium-sized carrot, coarsely chopped
- 5 cups water
- 1 cup dry white wine
- 1 cup chopped fresh tomatoes
- Lobster coral, mashed (if you have it)
- ½ teaspoon dried tarragon
- 2 sprigs parsley
- 1 bay leaf

Heat the oil in a heavy-bottomed 4- to 5-quart pot. Add the chopped shells and cook them for about 5 minutes over high heat, tossing them frequently. Add the leek, onion, garlic, celery and carrot. Stir. Reduce the heat to low, partially cover the pot and cook for 5 minutes longer. Add the water, wine, tomatoes, coral (if you have it) and herbs. Bring the mixture to a simmer. Partially cover the pot again and simmer the mixture for about 1 hour. It should not boil, but always maintain a slow bubble.

Strain the stock immediately (I pour it first through a colander into a large bowl, then strain it through a fine sieve back into the rinsed pot that was used to cook it). Let the stock cool to room temperature, then refrigerate or freeze it. If refrigerated, it should be used in a day or 2; if frozen, it should be used within 3 months.

AÏOLI
ABOUT 1 CUP

- 6 to 8 large garlic cloves, peeled, cut in half and bitter green sprouts removed
- ¾ teaspoon salt
- 2 egg yolks
- 1 cup extra-virgin olive oil

I love the garlicky bite of homemade aïoli with almost any kind of seafood, but it's particularly good with fish soups or as a side sauce for deep-fried seafood, especially squid.

This rich and thick mayonnaise-type sauce is best made in the traditional way—without the aid of a blender or food processor—if it is to have the flavour and consistency of the authentic Mediterranean sauce.

Place the garlic in a large warmed mortar or deep bowl. Sprinkle the garlic with the salt and set it aside for about 10 minutes. (The salt will help to soften the garlic.) Using a pestle, crush and mash the garlic together until it forms a smooth paste. Add the egg yolks, one at a time, and continue to mash and stir with the pestle until they are completely incorporated. A drop or 2 at a time, beat in the olive oil until about half of it has been incorporated. Beating constantly, add the remaining oil in a very thin stream. The finished sauce should resemble a thick mayonnaise.

CAPER SAUCE
ABOUT 2 CUPS

- 1 tablespoon unsalted butter
- 1 tablespoon all-purpose flour
- 1 cup fish stock (or substitute bottled clam juice diluted with water), heated to a simmer
- 1 tablespoon capers, drained
- 1 tablespoon freshly squeezed lemon juice
- Salt to taste

In a small heavy saucepan, melt the butter over moderate heat. When the foam subsides, stir in the flour and mix it thoroughly with the butter. Cook the mixture for about 1 minute over low heat, stirring constantly. Do not let the mixture brown. Remove the saucepan from the heat and pour in the simmering stock or clam juice all at once. Whisk to blend the ingredients well. Return the saucepan to high heat and, whisking constantly, continue to cook the sauce until it comes to a boil and is thick and smooth. Stir in the capers and lemon juice. Taste the sauce for seasoning and add salt if necessary. If the sauce must wait, keep it warm over a pan of simmering water and stir to recombine before serving.

Capers are the buds of a bush native to the Mediterranean and parts of Asia. The small buds are picked, dried and then pickled in brine or salted. Capers range in size from the petite variety from southern France (considered the finest), to those from Italy, which can be as large as the tip of your little finger. There are also caper berries with stems, usually imported from Spain, that are about the size of a small cocktail olive.

Capers should be rinsed before using to remove excess salt. I love the piquancy they lend to many fish dishes and seafood sauces.

CREAM SAUCE WITH SAFFRON AND FENNEL
ABOUT 1¼ CUPS

- ¼ cup finely minced shallots
- 4 sprigs parsley
- ½ small bay leaf
- 2 sprigs fresh thyme, or pinch dried thyme
- 1 clove garlic, mashed
- ¼ teaspoon crushed saffron threads
- ¼ teaspoon whole fennel seeds
- 1 cup dry white wine
- ½ cup bottled clam juice
- 2 tablespoons unsalted butter
- 2 tablespoons all-purpose flour
- 1 egg yolk
- ¼ cup heavy cream
- Salt and freshly ground pepper
- Lemon juice

This is a rich sauce, so a little goes a long way. It's a delicious way to turn simply prepared seafood into an elegant meal.

The sauce may be made an hour or so ahead of time and gently reheated before serving. If you wish to do this, place a round of buttered waxed paper directly on the surface of the sauce to prevent a skin from forming.

In a small non-reactive saucepan, combine the shallots, parsley, bay leaf, thyme, garlic, saffron and fennel. Pour in the wine and the clam juice. Bring the mixture to a boil over high heat and continue to boil for 10 minutes. Strain this stock through a fine sieve into a bowl, pressing down hard on the solids to extract all their flavour. Return the stock to the saucepan and boil it down again until it is reduced to ¾ cup. Keep the stock warm over low heat.

In a heavy 1-quart saucepan, melt the butter over moderately low heat. Add the flour and, stirring constantly, cook it for 2 minutes. Do not let it brown. Remove the pan from the heat and stir in the hot stock. Return the mixture to high heat and, stirring constantly with a whisk, cook it until it comes to a boil and is thick and smooth. Remove it from the heat.

In a bowl, mix the egg yolk with the cream. Stir 2 tablespoons of the hot sauce into the egg-yolk mixture. Pour the mixture back into the remaining sauce. Bring the sauce to a boil over moderate heat, whisking constantly, until it is thick enough to coat a spoon. Season the sauce to taste with salt, pepper and drops of lemon juice.

COCKTAIL SAUCE
ABOUT 1½ CUPS

- 1 small clove garlic
- 1 cup mayonnaise, preferably homemade (see recipe index)
- ½ cup prepared chili sauce
- 4 teaspoons drained bottled horseradish
- ½ teaspoon dry mustard
- ¼ teaspoon cayenne, or to taste
- 1 tablespoon freshly squeezed lemon juice

This is the classic sauce for chilled shrimp cocktail, but it also complements other cold shellfish, such as lobster and crab. Don't restrict it to chilled seafood, however, because it makes a great dipping sauce for deep-fried shrimp and other hot seafood appetizers.

Force the garlic through a garlic press into a medium-sized bowl. Stir in the mayonnaise, chili sauce, horseradish, mustard, cayenne and lemon juice. Taste and adjust the seasonings.

Chill the sauce for at least 4 hours before serving to allow the flavours to blend. The sauce will keep, tightly covered and refrigerated, for about 3 days.

Drawn Butter Sauce with Onion
About 2 Cups

- 2 medium-sized onions, finely chopped
- 2 cups cold water
- ¼ cup unsalted butter
- 1 tablespoon all-purpose flour
- ½ teaspoon salt
- ¼ teaspoon ground white pepper

In Newfoundland and Labrador, this sauce, or a version of it, is often served with plainly poached fish. It's always a favourite with cod, both fresh and salted.

If you wish a smoother sauce, it may be forced through a sieve before serving, but traditionally the bits of onion are left in it.

In a small heavy saucepan, combine the chopped onions with the cold water. Bring the mixture to a boil over high heat. Reduce the heat to low, cover the saucepan and simmer for about 20 minutes, or until the onions are very soft.

In a medium-sized heavy saucepan, melt the butter over moderate heat. When the foam subsides, stir in the flour and mix it thoroughly with the butter. Cook the mixture for about 1 minute over low heat, stirring constantly. Do not let it brown. Remove the saucepan from the heat and pour in the onion-and-water mixture all at once. Whisk to blend the ingredients well. Return the saucepan to high heat and, whisking constantly, continue to cook the sauce until it comes to a boil and is thick and smooth. Stir in the salt and pepper. Taste the sauce for seasoning and add more salt if necessary.

If the sauce must wait, keep it warm over a pan of simmering water and stir to recombine it before serving.

HERB ESSENCE SAUCE
ABOUT 2 CUPS

- ¼ cup finely chopped mixed fresh herbs, a combination of tarragon, chervil, chives and parsley (or substitute 2 tablespoons dried herbs)
- 1 cup dry white wine
- 3 tablespoon unsalted butter
- 3 tablespoons all-purpose flour
- 2 cups boiling basic fish stock (see recipe index)
- Drops of freshly squeezed lemon juice to taste
- Salt to taste

This is one of my favourite sauces. It's particularly good with salmon or trout. A variety of mild herbs simmered in white wine provides a complex burst of flavour. We enjoy this sauce most in summer when we have fresh herbs growing in our garden, but, out of season, I use dried herbs.

In a small heavy non-reactive saucepan, combine the wine and herbs. Bring the mixture to a boil over high heat. Reduce the heat to moderate and continue to boil the mixture, stirring occasionally, for 10 to 15 minutes, or until it is reduced to about 3 tablespoons. Remove the saucepan from the heat and set the herb essence aside.

In a medium-sized non-reactive saucepan, melt the butter over moderate heat. When the foam begins to subside, add the flour and, stirring constantly with a wire whisk, cook the mixture for about 2 minutes. Do not let it brown. Remove the butter and flour mixture from the heat and pour in the boiling fish stock all at once, whisking vigorously to incorporate it. Return the saucepan to high heat and continue whisking until the sauce comes to a boil and is thick and smooth. Stir in the herb essence and cook, stirring, for 1 minute longer. Add drops of lemon juice and salt to taste.

Herb essence sauce may be made several hours before serving, kept at room temperature and reheated. If you choose to do this, film the top with a thin layer of melted butter so that it does not form a skin. The butter will further enrich the sauce.

MAYONNAISE
ABOUT 2 CUPS

- 3 egg yolks, at room temperature
- 1 to 3 teaspoons freshly squeezed lemon juice
- ½ teaspoon dry mustard
- ½ teaspoon salt
- Small pinch ground white pepper
- 1½ cups olive oil
- 2 tablespoons boiling water

Warm a deep mixing bowl in hot water and dry it thoroughly. Drop in the egg yolks. Using a large balloon-type wire whisk or an electric beater, beat the egg yolks vigorously for several minutes, or until they are thick and light in colour.

Add 1 teaspoon of the lemon juice, the mustard, salt and pepper. Continue to beat to combine well. Begin beating in the olive oil, ½ teaspoon at a time, making sure each addition is fully absorbed before adding more. After about ½ cup of the oil has been beaten in, the sauce should be like thick cream. Add the rest of the oil in a very thin stream, beating constantly. Taste the mayonnaise and season with extra lemon juice, salt and pepper if necessary. To make the sauce creamier and lessen the danger of separation, beat in the boiling water by drops.

Transfer the mayonnaise to a jar or small bowl and cover it tightly. Refrigerated, the mayonnaise will keep for about a week.

Good-quality mayonnaise is delicious with many cold fish dishes and is always best if homemade. With the addition of other ingredients, mayonnaise also forms the base for other sauces.

I've never had much luck making mayonnaise in a food processor, perhaps because the bowl is too large for the small quantity of sauce. I prefer to make the mayonnaise by hand. However, I have made mayonnaise successfully in a blender. The method is the same, except that the oil is slowly dribbled in through the feed tube.

Mayonnaise is easiest to make when all the ingredients are at room temperature and the mixing bowl has been warmed.

RÉMOULADE SAUCE
ABOUT 1 CUP

- 1 tablespoon minced white onion
- 1 tablespoon minced celery
- 1 tablespoon minced green pepper
- ½ cup Creole-style mustard
- ¼ cup olive oil
- 1½ tablespoons red wine vinegar
- 1 tablespoon minced fresh parsley leaves
- 1 teaspoon paprika
- 2 teaspoons Worcestershire sauce
- 2 drops Tabasco or to taste
- ½ teaspoon salt
- ½ teaspoon white pepper

Rémoulade sauce is very easy to make and is excellent with almost any kind of fish or shellfish. It also makes a good sandwich spread for seafood fillings or may become a base for seafood canapés.

In a small deep bowl, stir together all the ingredients. Blend them well. Taste the sauce and adjust the seasonings.

Cover the bowl tightly with plastic wrap and refrigerate the *rémoulade* sauce for at least 2 hours before serving to allow the flavours to blend.

Tightly covered and refrigerated, the sauce will keep for 2 or 3 days.

ROUILLE
ABOUT 2 CUPS

- 1 large vine-ripened tomato
- 1 large red bell pepper
- 1 small potato, peeled and boiled until tender
- 1 cup mayonnaise, preferably homemade (see recipe index)
- ¼ cup heated fish stock, chicken stock or clam juice
- 6 cloves garlic, pushed through a garlic press
- Pinch saffron
- 2 to 4 drops hot pepper sauce, such as Tabasco
- Salt
- Freshly ground black pepper

Rouille is a classic garlicky sauce for bouillabaisse, but it makes any fish soup more splendid. It's also great on broiled or poached fish.

There are many versions of this sauce. Some include bread as a thickener and some add wine for tanginess. We prefer this version, thickened with a small potato and enhanced with a hint of saffron and a generous hit of hot pepper sauce.

Drop the tomato into boiling water to cover for about 30 seconds. Remove the tomato and peel off the skin, beginning at the stem end. Cut the tomato in half and remove the core and seeds. Coarsely chop the tomato and set it aside.

Set an oven rack about 4 inches from the broiler element and preheat the broiler.

Quarter the red bell pepper lengthwise, discarding the stem, seeds and ribs. Place the pepper quarters in a shallow pan, skin side up, and broil them until the skin is charred and blistered, about 10 minutes. Transfer the pepper quarters to a small bowl. Cover the bowl tightly with plastic wrap and let the pepper "sweat" for 5 minutes so it is easier to peel. Using a sharp knife, peel off the skin.

In a food processor or blender, purée the tomato, roasted pepper, potato, mayonnaise, fish stock, garlic and saffron. Transfer the mixture to a bowl. Stir in hot pepper sauce, salt and freshly ground pepper to taste. Refrigerate the sauce, covered, for at least 4 hours, and up to 3 days, to allow the flavours to blend.

TARTAR SAUCE

ABOUT ¾ CUP

- ½ cup mayonnaise, preferably homemade (see recipe index)
- 2 tablespoons minced fresh parsley leaves
- 2 tablespoons minced sweet pickles
- 1 tablespoon minced onion
- 1 tablespoon minced celery
- 1½ teaspoons Dijon-style mustard
- 1 teaspoon freshly squeezed lemon juice
- ½ teaspoon minced fresh tarragon leaves or ¼ teaspoon dried tarragon
- ¼ teaspoon celery seeds
- Tabasco or other hot pepper sauce to taste
- Salt to taste

Tartar sauce is commercially available, but your own homemade sauce will taste much fresher.

Tartar sauce is a traditional accompaniment to deep-fried fish and shellfish, but it also marries well with grilled or pan-fried seafood.

In a small deep bowl, stir together all the ingredients except the hot pepper sauce and salt. Blend well. Taste for seasoning and add the pepper sauce to taste and salt if necessary.

Cover the bowl tightly with plastic wrap and refrigerate the tartar sauce for at least 2 hours before serving to allow the flavours to blend. Tightly covered and refrigerated, the sauce will keep for several days.

TOMATO SAUCE
ABOUT 2 CUPS

- 1 small onion, finely chopped
- 2 large cloves garlic, minced
- 2 tablespoons extra-virgin olive oil
- 1½ pounds fresh vine-ripened tomatoes, peeled, cored and coarsely chopped, or 1 28-ounce can Italian plum tomatoes, including juice, coarsely chopped
- Pinch sugar
- ¼ teaspoon dried basil
- Pinch dried red pepper flakes
- Salt

This basic tomato sauce may be served as it is or extra herbs may be added. It's best when well-ripened fresh tomatoes are in season, but canned Italian plum tomatoes produce a fine sauce.

To peel fresh tomatoes, dunk them into boiling water to cover for a minute or so. The skins will slip off easily.

In a heavy saucepan, cook the onion and the garlic in the oil over moderate heat, stirring, until they just begin to turn golden, about 7 minutes. Add the tomatoes with their juice, sugar, basil, red pepper flakes and salt to taste. Simmer the sauce, uncovered, stirring occasionally, for about 20 minutes, or until it is thickened. Taste and adjust the seasonings.

The sauce may be made up to 2 days ahead of time and kept covered and refrigerated.

Sauce Velouté with Variations
About 1 Cup

- 2 tablespoons unsalted butter
- 2 tablespoons all-purpose flour
- 1 cup basic fish stock (see recipe index), heated to a simmer
- Salt
- Freshly ground pepper

Don't let the French name deter you. Sauce Velouté is a simple white sauce made with fish stock and a roux, a mixture of butter and flour. Made with carefully seasoned fish stock, this a good basic sauce for many fish and shellfish dishes. With the addition of a few other ingredients, it becomes a different sauce with a different name. I've given a few variations, but I'm sure you'll come up with some of your own.

In a heavy 1-quart saucepan, melt the butter over moderately low heat. Add the flour and, stirring constantly, cook it for 2 minutes. Do not let it brown. Remove the pan from the heat and stir in the hot stock. Return the mixture to high heat and, stirring constantly with a whisk, cook it until it comes to a boil and is thick and smooth. Season the sauce to taste with salt and pepper.

Rich Velouté
Blend 1 cup of light cream with 2 egg yolks. Gradually whisk in about 3 tablespoons of the hot basic sauce. Then whisk the egg-yolk mixture back into the remaining sauce and continue to whisk over moderately low heat until slightly thickened.

Sauce Mornay
Let the basic sauce cool for a minute or 2. Then whisk in ¼ cup of grated Swiss cheese and a pinch of nutmeg.

Sauce Aurore
Add ¼ cup of tomato paste and ¼ cup heavy cream to the basic sauce.

Curry Sauce
Let the basic sauce cool for a minute or 2. Then add ½ cup of light cream and 1 to 2 teaspoons of curry powder.

Sauce Soubise
Add ½ cup of finely minced shallots or onions, sautéed, but not browned.

MUSTARD SAUCE
ABOUT 2 CUPS

- 6 tablespoons unsalted butter, softened
- 3 tablespoons all-purpose flour
- 2 cups basic fish stock (see recipe index), heated to a simmer
- 1 egg yolk
- 2 tablespoons heavy cream
- Salt
- Freshly ground pepper
- 1 to 2 tablespoons freshly squeezed lemon juice
- 2 tablespoons Dijon-type prepared mustard

This quickly made sauce does not belong to the velouté family of sauces because it begins with an uncooked roux (butter and flour mixture). It's a wonderful sauce for broiled mackerel or herring, but it also flatters tuna or swordfish. In place of plain Dijon mustard, you could use purchased mustard that is flavoured with herbs or other ingredients that suit your taste.

In a heavy 1-quart saucepan, using a rubber spatula, blend together 2 tablespoons of the softened butter with the flour. Whisk in the simmering stock, blending thoroughly.

In a medium-sized bowl, blend together the egg yolk and cream with a wire whip. A few drops at a time, beat in ½ cup of the sauce. Beat in the rest of the sauce in a thin stream. Pour the mixture back into the saucepan and bring it to a boil over moderately high heat,

whisking constantly for a few seconds, or until the sauce is smooth. Remove the sauce from the heat and season it to taste with salt, pepper and lemon juice. Set the sauce aside, partially covered.

In a small bowl, blend together the mustard and remaining 4 tablespoons of softened butter. Just before serving, reheat the sauce gently and stir in the mustard-butter mixture, about 1 teaspoon at a time, until well blended.

FLAVOURED BUTTERS
ABOUT ½ CUP

- ½ cup unsalted butter, at room temperature
- Seasonings of choice

Simple to make, flavoured butters are especially recommended for grilled or broiled fish or shellfish. These butters can be refrigerated and stored for at least a week. I like to roll the seasoned butter into a log shape and chill it tightly wrapped in waxed paper. Then the butter may be cut into neat pats to melt over a portion of seafood.

In a large bowl, beat the butter with a wooden spoon until it is very light and fluffy. Beat in the chosen seasonings.

GARLIC BUTTER
Add 1 to 2 cloves garlic, puréed with a mortar and pestle or pushed through a garlic press. Add 1 tablespoon of finely minced parsley and salt to taste

LEMON BUTTER
Whisk 2 tablespoons of lemon juice into the softened butter. Add a little paprika and salt to taste.

MINTED BUTTER
Add 1 tablespoon of lemon juice and 2 tablespoons of finely chopped mint leaves. Season the mixture with salt to taste. (Note that other herbs, such as basil, tarragon or parsley, or a mixture of several herbs, may be used.)

SHALLOT BUTTER
Add 1 tablespoon of finely minced shallots and 1 tablespoon of white wine vinegar. Season the mixture with salt and pepper to taste.

INDEX